Just
Eat
Real
Food

30-minute nutrient-dense meals
for a healthy, balanced life

Just
Eat
Real
Food

Caitlin Greene
founder of star infinite food

PAGE STREET
PUBLISHING CO.

PAGE STREET
PUBLISHING CO.

First published in 2021 by
Page Street Publishing Co.
27 Congress Street, Suite 105
Salem, MA 01970
www.pagestreetpublishing.com

Distributed by Macmillan, sales in Canada by The Canadian Manda Group.

25   24   23   22   21   1   2   3   4   5

ISBN-13: 978-1-64567-223-4
ISBN-10: 1-64567-223-9

Library of Congress Control Number: 2020944072

Cover and book design by Kylie Alexander for Page Street Publishing Co.
Photography by Caitlin Greene

Printed and bound in China

As you get into these recipes, keep in mind that eating "healthy" and "wholesome" doesn't mean sticking to a rigid definition. Let's keep it relaxed and leave some wiggle room. For me, healthy eating does not mean avoiding or eliminating your favorite foods. Instead, it means making easy, nutrient-dense swaps; accommodating common food allergies and dietary preferences; and utilizing a variety of whole foods to do so. Fueling myself with real food every day creates a sustainable and satisfied feeling in my body, my mind and my spirit. I want that for you, too!

One more thing to consider: Preparing healthy and wholesome dishes doesn't have to take all day. I think we can all agree that time is precious. We are all busy. Life is constantly moving. Flexibility is crucial. I hear a lot from my followers that they wish they could make nutritious meals, but they just don't have the time. "Eating healthy is too complicated." Nonsense! These recipes are intended to make the process easy for you and just as convenient as it is to drive down the street to grab takeout. All you have to do is stock your pantry and refrigerator, and I'll show you the way.

Let's dispel the belief that eating healthy means eating salads and green juices daily. I have rounded up a collection of some of my favorite meals, including ideas for breakfast, appetizers, entrées, sides and desserts. I am sharing with you my (not-so-secret) methods that save time without compromising flavor. Every recipe can be made in under 30 minutes, and with a wide variety of flavors, so you'll never have a dull meal.

I have timed the recipes in this book to be "oven-to-table" ready in 30 minutes or less. I have not included time to prep vegetables (washing, chopping, mincing, etc.) or to preheat the oven, but instead have listed the ingredients as prepared (e.g., chopped onion instead of whole onion).

A simple time-saver for me is to prep vegetables ahead of time, such as chopping onions, mincing garlic and washing vegetables before storing them. I typically do this after I grocery shop on the weekends. That way, when the time comes to cook dinner or prepare lunch, I can dive right in. Of course, you can also do so before you begin making a recipe, just be sure to add a few minutes to the total time. Alternatively, you could opt to purchase pre-chopped vegetables for the recipes in this book. As for preheating the oven, I like to do this when I begin gathering ingredients, then I gather the necessary tools (bowls, blender, pans, etc.) and by the time the food is prepped for the oven, the oven is ready to go!

Enjoy cooking, and make your meals a celebration. Find joy in the satisfaction of healthful sustenance! Go forth and make magic with real food, every day.

FAQs About Eating Real Food Every Day

Q: **Are you vegan, vegetarian, Paleo, gluten-free and/or dairy-free?**

A: I personally don't follow any strict diet, except a gluten-free one because I can't tolerate gluten. I try to minimize my dairy intake, but I don't eliminate it completely. When I use dairy, I opt for grass-fed and raw (cheese).

My food philosophy overall is to "seek balance and use whole foods." I don't count calories. I try to stay mindful of portions and listen to my hunger cues. Some days, I eat more plant-based; other days, I eat more animal-based.

Q: **What basic tools does a foodie need to be successful in the kitchen?**

A: Here is a list of my top essential kitchen tools:

- One good, solid, sharp knife
- One good serrated knife
- Saucepans in a few different sizes—at least one small and one large. I prefer cast iron. I don't like to use nonstick pans, as the coating eventually breaks down and releases toxins.
- One or two wood cutting boards
- Measuring spoons
- Liquid measuring cups and solid measuring cups (there is a difference)
- Wooden spoon(s), spatula and whisk
- Food processor
- Hand grater
- Electric hand mixer or stand mixer (optional)

- Mixing bowls of a few different sizes
- Two sheet pans
- One muffin pan and/or loaf pan

Q: **What are your favorite kitchen tools to make it easier to cook real food every day?**

A: Here are the tools I recommend:

- **Air fryer:** I use my Ninja® Foodi™ Grill (it has multiple functions) daily.
- **Pressure cooker:** This is really good to have for making things that you would typically make in a slow cooker, but much faster. I recommend Ninja or Instant Pot®.
- **Quality blender:** You can get a high-speed blender of good quality for about $200. The cost justifies the result of the food blending and texture. If you want one that is going to not only get great results, but also last, you'll be spending between $400 and $600. I recommend a Blendtec®.
- **Immersion blender:** One of these is good to have, especially if you don't already have a quality high-speed blender. This works well for soups and sauces.
- **Ice-cream maker:** You can make your own flavors using ingredients that work for you. I recommend Cuisinart®.
- **Stand mixer:** If you're baking and making dough, it saves your manpower and mixes ingredients together well. I recommend KitchenAid®.
- **Kitchen scale:** Makes portioning easy, and I swear by it for baking. Any inexpensive scale will do.

Q: Is it better to purchase two great knives of quality or purchase a less expensive knife set that is complete?

A: You should always have on hand one great sharp knife and one great serrated knife. I recommend spending money on a good-quality knife, as opposed to a cheap set. I cooked for years without a good knife. It makes the process longer and the cuts less precise. You're also more likely to cut yourself! Spend the money and invest in building your kitchen tool set for quality over time, if budget is a concern.

Q: What is your preferred method of frying for a healthier option?

A: Air frying, using an air fryer appliance, is my go-to. You'll get the crispy outside and the moist inside similar to deep-frying in oil—but without the oil. It's the new, healthier way to fry food that doesn't sacrifice taste and is much less messy.

Q: How do you clean cast iron?

A: Never scrub cast iron with soap and a sponge! Simply let the piece cool, then clean it with water. If there is any food residue on the surface, leave the pan to soak in water and baking soda. Then, scrub with coarse sea salt to get rid of anything stuck to the surface. Using the baking soda and salt cleaning method, I have revived pans over 60 years old!

After you're done cleaning, always reseason it (you will also need to season it when you first buy it). Seasoning the pan strengthens and builds up a nonstick surface over time. Wipe out and blot away all the water. Then, use a paper towel and a neutral cooking oil, such as olive or avocado oil, to wipe over the surface of the pan. This will keep it moisturized. Avoid cooking acidic foods, such as tomatoes, as these can remove the pan's oil-derived nonstick coating.

Cast iron should literally last forever if you take care of it. You can often find good inexpensive pans (if you live in the US) at TJ Maxx and HomeGoods. Sometimes, you can snag some good finds at yard sales.

Q: How do I manage storing leftovers and batch-cooked foods?

A: For leftovers and meal prepping, I use glass food storage containers, which you can find in various sizes with different kinds of lids. They can be used to meal prep individual meals after batch cooking for the week, and they can be stored easily in the freezer. I also use Mason jars to store sauces, prepared salads and even prepared veggies. Mason jars are a great vessel for storing homemade nut milks and oils (such as homemade ghee; see page 14). They are an inexpensive way to store leftovers and freeze soups and sauces as well (just never fill to the very top when freezing sauce and soup, because liquids expand when frozen).

For sandwiches and other "baggable" items, I like to use Stasher Bags made from silicone, which can be reused.

Q: What are the most valuable real food ingredients I should stock in my kitchen?

A: I always try to have these ingredients on hand:

- Coconut aminos, liquid aminos
- Apple cider vinegar
- Himalayan pink salt, sea salt
- Grass-fed butter, olive oil, coconut oil
- Lemons, limes
- Nut butter, tahini
- Honey, pure maple syrup, coconut sugar, stevia
- Coconut, almond and gluten-free flour; oats
- Frozen fish, meat, eggs
- Fresh herbs
- Fresh and frozen vegetables
- 2 or 3 fresh fruits, frozen fruits
- Onions, garlic
- Unsweetened cocoa powder, chocolate chips, dark chocolate

- Dairy-free milk (I prefer coconut, cashew or almond milk)
- Bone broth (I get mine frozen)
- Gluten-free bread, tortillas
- Plain (unsweetened) yogurt (dairy or nondairy)

Q: I have nut allergies—do some recipes that call for nuts have replacement equivalents?

A: You can always omit the nuts in a recipe that includes them as a topping, or use sunflower or pumpkin seeds if you want that crunch as a replacement. For recipes that use nut butters, I recommend using either tahini or sunflower seed butter, as they will work in a similar manner. Silken tofu can also sometimes work to replace raw cashews in a sauce.

Q: What type of salt do you recommend?

A: I always use either Himalayan pink salt or sea salt. These salts are less refined, and they have a milder flavor. They are also loaded with beneficial minerals. All the recipes in this book were tested with one of these salts.

Q: How do you store avocado for future use?

A: Put the leftover avocado, still in its peel, into a lidded container and add the removed peel and pit. Store it in the fridge and it should stay good for a few days. When ready to eat it, simply cut the brown part off. If you ever cut open an avocado too soon and it's really hard, place it in the fridge. After a few days, it will ripen and still be green. Ripe avocados can also be frozen until ready to use!

Q: Do you have tips on how to accelerate banana ripening?

A: If you want bananas to ripen faster, put them in a paper bag and keep them in a higher-elevated area in your home. The lack of air and the higher tempera-ture (at a higher elevation, heat rises) brings out the sweetness of the banana. This works for most fruits, including avocado.

If you want to use a cheater method for bananas, because you want to make banana bread right away, put the bananas in the oven set to a low heat (300°F [150°C]) for about 20 minutes, or until the peel turns brown. Remove from the oven and let cool.

Q: Why are bananas used in so many vegan recipes, and is there a substitute?

A: Bananas are used in a lot of baked goods because they can act as a stabilizer, just as an egg does, and add moisture. Most of my recipes don't include bananas because although I love bananas, their flavor is powerful. Whatever you're making with banana is always going to taste like banana.

If you are looking for a similar replacement for banana in vegan recipes, you can use ripe plantain, which has a milder flavor. If you are looking to substitute for the moisture banana can bring to recipes, applesauce can be used. If banana is being used as a replacement for egg, you can try using ground chia seeds or flaxseeds mixed with water (see page 14 for more on chia and flax eggs).

Q: What is the benefit of using grass-fed or raw milk products?

A: Grass-fed or raw milk products are less processed and the result is that they are higher in beneficial fatty acids as well as antioxidants. The flavor is better, in my opinion.

Q: How can I make my own nut butters to save money if I buy nuts in bulk?

A: Place your nuts of choice, raw or roasted, in a food processor or high-speed blender. Add vanilla extract, ground cinnamon or salt, if desired, a little oil, if you like, then just blend until smooth. You can also do this with seeds: pumpkin, sunflower, etc. Just make sure the blender or food processor is powerful.

Q: **What is ghee and can I make it at home?**

A: Ghee, also called clarified butter, is essentially butter with the milk protein removed. It is lactose-free, but not dairy-free as it is originally a milk-derived product. For people who are sensitive to lactose, ghee is a more suitable option.

To make your own ghee, heat 1 pound (455 g) of unsalted butter (I recommend grass-fed) in a pan over medium to medium-low heat for 15 to 20 minutes. It will foam again and again. Eventually, the milk proteins will brown at the top. Remove the pan from the heat at this point and strain through a mesh strainer. The milk proteins will stay in the strainer, and you will be left with a golden liquid: ghee. You can store it in a jar at room temperature.

Q: **What are aminos and what do they help with in a recipe? Is there a kind you use a lot?**

A: I use coconut aminos and liquid aminos. Both are commonly used as a soy sauce substitute. I prefer liquid aminos when I want to include that salty soy flavor. Coconut aminos are also slightly salty, but they have a bit of sweetness to them and add umami to a recipe. I use coconut aminos to balance out flavors in sauces and other recipes. I also replace Worcestershire sauce with coconut aminos, which have a similar taste. I also sometimes call for tamari, a wheat-free form of soy sauce suitable for gluten-free cooking (regular soy sauce contains wheat).

Q: **How long do your recipes stay good for?**

A: **Meat-based protein and soups after being cooked:** 3 to 4 days at most. Otherwise, I freeze them.

Shellfish: 1 to 2 days. Other seafood: up to 3 days.

Sauces and dips without dairy: about 1 week. If a sauce has dairy or yogurt: 3 to 4 days.

Baked goods: 5 to 7 days in the fridge. Typically I freeze extra baked goods, including breakfast foods such as pancakes.

Q: **Do you have an egg substitute for those who have allergies to eggs?**

A: One chia seed or flaxseed "egg" = 1 egg. To make a vegan chia or flaxseed egg, mix 1 tablespoon (10 or 12 g) of ground chia seeds or ground flaxseeds with 3 tablespoons (45 ml) of water. Let it sit for 5 minutes and it will gel up. Please note, I can't always guarantee this method will create the same consistency as using egg. Alternatively, try:

- ½ cup (113 g) mashed banana or plantain = 1 egg
- ¼ cup (60 g) applesauce = 1 egg
- 3 tablespoons (48 g) nut butter = 1 egg
- 2 to 3 tablespoons (28 to 42 g) mashed potatoes or mashed sweet potato = 1 egg
- 1 tablespoon (10 g) beef gelatin powder mixed with 3 tablespoons (45 ml) water = 1 egg
- Certain brands, including Bob's Red Mill, carry egg replacement products.

Q: **Can I substitute other flours in a recipe if I do not like the grain suggested or have a sensitivity? Will that impact the recipe or end result?**

A: It depends on what you are trying to replace. Different flours have different amounts of protein and fiber.

Oat flour, millet flour, sorghum flour, quinoa flour and buckwheat flour are all higher-fiber flours and can be somewhat interchangeable.

However, coconut flour doesn't work like a typical flour. It cooks very differently and requires a certain amount of moisture, eggs and possibly other ingredients to turn out right. Similar can be said for almond flour. If you are following a recipe that calls for coconut or almond flour, don't try substituting a different flour, as the item probably will not turn out as desired.

Q: What is your view on sweeteners and sugar substitutes, such as stevia and monk fruit?

A: As you will find in this book, I mostly use unrefined sweeteners to add sweetness to recipes: coconut sugar, pure maple syrup, honey and dates. If I am going to use cane sugar, I use unrefined cane sugar. It is slightly less processed than white table sugar.

As for stevia and monk fruit, I do use them in moderation. Although they are from natural sources, they can cause digestion disruption and oftentimes have extra additives. Some people don't like the aftertaste. I don't mind it, but I wouldn't use a lot of it on a daily basis.

Q: How can I make fresh herbs and produce last longer?

A: Store the herbs in spring water in mason jars in the fridge. Use just enough water to cover a couple of inches of the stems. I do this with soft-leafed herbs, such as parsley, cilantro and dill, as well as such vegetables as asparagus, broccolini and kale. When it comes to such herbs as rosemary and thyme, I store those in a dry container in the fridge.

For scallions: Cut the tips of the dark green tops off, then place the scallions in a jar with water covering the roots and place them in the sun, as they will continue to grow. Change the water every couple of days to maintain freshness at the roots.

For such veggies as carrots and celery: Store them completely submerged in water in a glass container in the fridge and they can last up to a few months. I change the water every week to maintain freshness.

Q: Can I make my own dairy-free milk?

A: It's easy to make your own dairy-free milks and is much more affordable than buying them prepared. All you need is a blender and whatever the base ingredient is; for example, oats for oat milk, coconut for coconut milk and so on.

In a food processor, combine 4 cups (960 ml) of spring water with 1 cup (80 g) of nuts or oats (or whatever your desired base ingredient is), process until a milk is created, then strain the solids.

In a pinch, I blend water with nut butter. Typically it's about 1 tablespoon (16 g) of nut butter to make 1 cup (240 ml) of nut milk. You can add flavorings or sweetener of your choice.

Q: Any additional storage tips that you swear by?

A: For flour that you may not use quickly, it's best to freeze it. Especially if you buy in bulk. This keeps it from going rancid.

Be sure to store onions and potatoes separately.

Store dry goods, such as granola, nuts, rice and pasta, in Mason jars, which saves on clutter from open boxes or bags and keeps them fresh longer.

I store bananas and avocados separate from my other fruits, as they tend to ripen quickly and unevenly when crowded.

ENERGY-LIFTING
Meals

"I'm making my signature smoked salmon platter and Colleen is making a cheesecake. Who wants to be in charge of the protein?" I jump in to respond, "I'll do it, but I'm doing a surf and turf: curried lamb meatballs and shrimp bisque." It's become a ritual when my family gets together to create a menu as a group. The result: an unspoken playful competition among the family dishes.

Growing up in a family of chefs was a blessing. From a young age, I was exposed to a variety of unique cooking styles, but there is one common thread: We all can make a five-star meal out of just about anything. My dad was a master griller and he taught me the best of his skills. My mom—she can make anything taste delicious, and I've used many of her recipes as inspiration for my own. My brothers both went to culinary school and my sister had her own bakery business for years. As the youngest, I was able to learn from everyone. They taught me to be the best. I pay reverence to all of my family for showing me the ropes, and it's funny that now they pay reverence to me, the little one, for bypassing them and making a career in food.

Over time, I developed my own unique style of cooking. I thrive on re-creating my childhood and restaurant favorites and inventing dishes in a lighter fashion by infusing flavor with whole foods, fresh herbs and nourishing spices. That's exactly what you'll find celebrated in this chapter—all kinds of delicious family-favorite comfort foods, made lighter and cleaner. I use such ingredients as mushrooms and cauliflower in place of bread crumbs, as you'll find in my Lamb Curry Meatballs (page 32)—one of my personal all-time favorite recipes. A suggestion for you: Instead of ordering Chinese takeout, try my Asian Beef and Broccoli (page 27). You'll get the same sweet, salty and umami flavors without all the additives, as well as bonus digestive support from the fresh ginger.

Grab some chicken breast, and in just 25 minutes, you can enjoy my Italian remake, Creamy Tuscan Chicken (page 31)—without the dairy! I'll even teach you how to make a mouthwatering Shrimp Bisque (page 35) right in your own kitchen in less than 30 minutes. Depending on what you or your family have a hankering for, I guarantee you'll find equally comforting and nourishing dinner inspiration for any night of the week.

Broiled Dijon Salmon

Paleo / Whole 30 / Gluten Free / Dairy Free / Nut Free / Keto

If you follow me on Instagram, you will see I have a plethora of recipes using salmon. This dish is a twist on the first salmon recipe I created. We bake then broil the salmon with a creamy, lightened-up aioli infused with mustard and fresh thyme. The aioli acts as a barrier, preventing the salmon from drying out, and as it reduces, the salmon absorbs the mustard and thyme notes. The result is a succulent piece of fish that melts in your mouth, all done in only 15 minutes. I find it pairs well with some steamed asparagus and fresh tomatoes to balance the richness.

Prep Time: 10 minutes
Cook Time: 10 minutes
Total Time: 20 minutes
Serves: 4

Preheat the oven to 400°F (200°C). Line a sheet pan with aluminum foil.

Place the salmon on the prepared sheet pan, pat it dry with a paper towel, season it with salt and pepper and set aside to get to room temperature while you prepare the aioli.

Make the aioli: In a food processor, combine the egg yolk and lemon juice and turn on the machine. Add a few drops of olive oil through the lid opening and let the processor run for a few seconds. Then, add a few more drops, and repeat until the mixture begins to thicken. Alternatively, begin adding a stream with the oil while the processor is running, until the oil is all added. It should continue to thicken during this process.

Scrape the aioli into a bowl. Add the thyme, ½ teaspoon of salt, ½ teaspoon of pepper, the Dijon, mustard seeds and garlic. Whisk to combine.

Spread the aioli evenly over the salmon. You may have a little left over, but be sure the salmon is covered. Bake on the bottom rack of the oven for 7 to 8 minutes, until the fish flakes easily with a fork and is cooked through. If the portion is very thick, bake it for 8 minutes.

After 8 minutes, turn on the broiler and place the salmon about 6 inches (15 cm) from the heat. Broil for about 1½ minutes, or until the salmon is golden on top. Serve the salmon with chopped chives and the veggies of your liking.

1 lb (455 g) salmon
Salt and freshly ground black pepper
1 large egg yolk
Squeeze of fresh lemon juice
½ cup (120 ml) olive oil
1 tsp fresh thyme leaves
2 tbsp (22 g) Dijon mustard
½ tsp mustard seeds
1 clove garlic, minced
Chopped chives or parsley, for garnish (optional)
Veggies, for serving

Meyer Lemon–Garlic Shrimp

Paleo / Whole 30 / Egg Free / Gluten Free
Dairy-Free Option / Nut Free / Keto

Meyer lemons are my favorite type of lemon. They are a cross between a mandarin orange and a lemon. They have a slight sweetness. Shrimp are slightly sweet by nature, absorb a lot of flavor, are easy to cook and are a great lean source of protein. I use ghee in this dish, keeping it lactose-free while still creating a buttery flavor. The addition of coconut aminos adds an umami component that complements the acidity of the lemon. The recipe requires very little effort and only 15 minutes of your time, but I always receive compliments on this one.

Prep Time: 10 minutes
Cook Time: 8 minutes
Total Time: 18 minutes
Serves: 4

Pat the shrimp dry with a paper towel, then toss them with the salt.

In a large skillet, heat the ghee over medium-high heat. After 1 minute, add the garlic and cook for 30 seconds, or until fragrant. Add the shrimp and sauté for 2 minutes.

Add the pepper, lemon juice and coconut aminos to the pan. Toss the shrimp with the liquid, lower the heat to medium and cook for another 3 minutes, or until the liquid has reduced.

Turn off the heat and toss the shrimp with the parsley, lemon zest and red pepper flakes. Serve with veggies, rice, pasta or on their own.

Note: If you cannot find Meyer lemons, regular lemons can be substituted.

1 lb (455 g) medium shrimp, fresh or thawed, peeled

½ tsp salt

1½ tbsp (21 g) ghee or coconut oil (use oil for dairy-free)

3 cloves garlic, minced

½ tsp freshly ground black pepper

3 tbsp (45 ml) fresh Meyer lemon juice

1½ tbsp (22 ml) coconut aminos

¼ cup (15 g) chopped fresh parsley

Meyer lemon zest, for garnish

Red pepper flakes, for garnish

Veggies, rice or pasta, for serving

Lemon-Fennel Monkfish

Paleo / Whole 30 / Egg Free / Gluten Free
Dairy-Free Option / Nut Free / Keto

This dish was inspired by a tasty swordfish recipe I came across in the *New York Times* featuring crushed fennel seeds, fresh lemon and garlic. I adapted it for monkfish. If you have never had monkfish, it is often referred to as the "poor man's lobster," as the texture is meaty and similar to that of a lobster tail, but with the delicate flavor of white fish. It is inexpensive and has the ability to absorb flavor. If you cannot find monkfish, this recipe works very well with halibut or mahi-mahi. This one-pan meal is easy to complete in less than 25 minutes and will impress your guests.

Prep Time: 15 minutes
Cook Time: 8 minutes
Total Time: 23 minutes
Serves: 3 or 4

Pat the fish dry, then season with salt and pepper. Set aside.

Using a sharp knife, carefully crush the fennel seeds using the back of the knife, then mince them with the blade to release their flavor, breaking the seeds into a coarse powder.

In a skillet large enough to hold all the fish cubes in one layer, heat the olive oil and butter over medium heat until the butter melts.

Add the diced fennel bulb and fish to the pan and allow to cook, turning the fish and basting it with the oil and butter, for 3 minutes.

Stir in the garlic, fennel seeds, lemon zest, ½ teaspoon of salt and the red pepper flakes, and continue to cook, stirring gently so as not to break up the fish cubes, until the fish is just cooked through, 3 to 4 minutes.

Gently stir in the lemon juice and coconut aminos. Garnish with the fennel fronds and lemon wedges. Serve over salad, pasta or veggies of your choice.

1 lb (455 g) monkfish steaks, cut into 1" (2.5-cm) cubes

Kosher salt and freshly ground black pepper

½ tsp fennel seeds

1½ tsp (scant 8 ml) olive oil

2 tsp (10 g) unsalted butter, ghee or coconut oil (use oil for dairy-free)

¼ cup (23 g) diced fennel bulb

2 cloves garlic, minced (about 1 tsp)

¼ tsp lemon zest

¼ tsp crushed red pepper flakes, or more to taste

1 tbsp (15 ml) fresh lemon juice

1 tbsp (15 ml) coconut aminos

¼ tsp chopped fresh fennel fronds, for serving

Lemon wedges, for serving

Salad, pasta or veggies, for serving

Lemony White Bean and Kale-Stuffed Sweet Potatoes

Egg Free / Gluten Free / Dairy Free / Vegan

I have found in my career as a chef that it is hard to come by vegan meals that everyone can enjoy. This recipe is exciting for me because the filling incorporates one of my favorite ways to prepare kale, with lots of lemon. With the protein-packed white bean and almond mix, this dish can be a balanced stand-alone meal, and it is truly a plant-oriented delight. Sweet potatoes typically take a fair amount of time to bake, but with my method, this dish is ready to enjoy in just 30 minutes.

Preheat the oven to 450°F (230°C).

Slice the sweet potatoes in half lengthwise. Brush 1 tablespoon (15 ml) of the olive oil on all sides of the potatoes. Place them in the oven, skin side up, directly on the rack with a cookie sheet underneath in case the sweet potatoes start to ooze. Bake for 25 minutes, flipping at about the 13-minute point. They should be fork-tender. Note that if you are using larger sweet potatoes, you may need to add more time to bake.

While the potatoes are baking, make the filling: In a large skillet, heat 1 tablespoon (15 ml) of the olive oil over medium-high heat. Add the onion and sauté for 2 to 3 minutes, or until it begins to soften and brown. Lower the heat to medium. Add the garlic and sun-dried tomatoes and toss to combine. Sauté for 3 minutes, or until fragrant.

Add the last tablespoon (15 ml) of olive oil and the kale, then toss to combine. Add the salt, pepper, paprika, lemon zest and thyme, and toss again. Add 2 tablespoons (30 ml) of stock and cook for 2 to 3 minutes, or until the kale has begun to soften a bit and the liquid has reduced. Add the remaining ¼ cup (60 ml) of stock and the coconut aminos, white beans and walnuts, and gently incorporate into the kale mixture, carefully as not to crush the beans. Lower the heat to medium-low, cover with a lid or aluminum foil and cook for 8 to 10 minutes, or until the kale is tender. Remove from the heat.

Remove the sweet potatoes from the oven and transfer to a plate. Cut a slice about 1 inch (2.5 cm) deep, lengthwise, into the potatoes and gently pull apart to create a boat shape with an area for the filling. Spoon equal amounts (about ½ cup [120 g]) of filling into each potato. Serve, drizzled with some tahini, if you wish.

Prep Time: 5 minutes
Cook Time: 25 minutes
Total Time: 30 minutes
Makes: 6 sweet potato halves (3 meals or 6 sides)

3 medium-sized sweet potatoes (each 3" to 4" [7.5 to 10 cm] long)

3 tbsp (45 ml) olive oil, divided

1 Vidalia onion, sliced

3 cloves garlic, chopped

1 tbsp (3 g) chopped dry sun-dried tomatoes (not in oil)

1 bunch kale, washed, stemmed and chopped (about 2 cups [134 g])

½ tsp salt

¼ tsp freshly ground black pepper

¼ tsp paprika

1 tsp lemon zest

½ tsp fresh thyme leaves

¼ cup (60 ml) plus 2 tbsp (30 ml) veggie stock, divided

2 tsp (10 ml) coconut aminos

1 (15-oz [425-g]) can white beans, drained and rinsed

2 tbsp (15 g) chopped walnuts

Tahini, for drizzling (optional)

Asian Beef and Broccoli

Paleo / Whole 30 / Egg Free / Gluten Free / Dairy Free / Nut Free

In college, living in Allston, Massachusetts, I was surrounded by Asian restaurants and quickly fell in love with beef and broccoli. When I learned of my gluten intolerance, I developed this recipe, which is quite simple and healthier than the traditional Chinese American version, but captures the essence of its flavor. I like using sirloin or flat-iron cuts here, because they maintain a tender consistency when sautéed. In under 30 minutes, while everyone is waiting for their delivery, you will be enjoying my better-for-you take on this classic.

Prep Time: 15 minutes
Cook Time: 12 minutes
Total Time: 27 minutes
Serves: 3 or 4

Begin the beef and broccoli: Cut the beef into ½-inch (1.3-cm)-thick slices, pat dry and season with the salt and pepper. Place them in a bowl and toss with the vinegar, coconut aminos, garlic and ginger. Set aside.

Make the sauce: In a separate small bowl, combine the coconut aminos, date, tapioca flour, sesame oil, fish sauce, vinegar, lime juice and red pepper flakes. Whisk together and set aside.

In a medium-sized saucepan, bring the water to a boil. Stir the broccoli florets into the water, and cook for 45 seconds. Drain and set aside.

Add the coconut oil to the saucepan and heat over medium-high heat. Once the oil is hot, add the beef in a single layer and cook until browned, usually about 30 seconds. Add the scallions and cook about 30 seconds more, tossing the beef with the scallions. Next, add the sauce and mix to combine. Heat until the sauce thickens, about a minute. Lastly, add the broccoli to the beef mixture and toss again.

Top the dish with more scallions, red pepper flakes and sesame seeds, if you wish. Serve with rice, cauliflower rice or noodles of choice.

Beef and Broccoli

1 lb (455 g) beef, such as sirloin or flat-iron

1¼ tsp (8 g) salt

¼ tsp freshly ground black pepper

1 tbsp (15 ml) apple cider vinegar

1 tsp coconut aminos

3 cloves garlic, minced

1½ tbsp (9 g) minced fresh ginger

3 cups (710 ml) water

1 medium-sized broccoli head, chopped into florets

1 tbsp (14 g) coconut oil

1 tbsp (6 g) chopped scallions, plus more for garnish (optional)

Sauce

¼ cup (60 ml) coconut aminos

1 date, pitted and chopped

1½ tsp (4 g) tapioca flour

1 tbsp (15 ml) sesame oil

1 tsp Asian fish sauce

1 tsp apple cider vinegar

1 tsp fresh lime juice

Pinch of red pepper flakes, plus more for garnish (optional)

Sesame seeds, for garnish (optional)

Rice, cauliflower rice or noodles of choice, for serving

Herbed Fish Cakes with Roasted Red Pepper Sauce

Paleo / Whole 30 / Gluten Free / Dairy Free / Keto

Being from New England, I could not leave out a quality fish cake recipe. These fish cakes have a better ratio of fish to bread crumb than you typically find. In fact, I don't use bread crumbs at all. We also bake the fish cakes, and they are done with only 10 minutes of prep time. My fish cakes are gluten-free and Paleo-friendly, since I use almond flour. I also incorporate a combination of fresh herbs and spices to complement the delicate white fish. Served with a creamy roasted red pepper dip, these flavorful fish cakes are assured to be a hit.

Preheat the oven to 400°F (200°C). Line a sheet pan with parchment paper and set aside.

Using a paper towel or cheesecloth, squeeze as much liquid as possible from the cod. Cut the cod into large chunks and set aside.

In a food processor, process the onion for 15 to 20 seconds, or until it is well chopped. Add the cod and process for about 20 more seconds. It should form a sticky mixture.

Transfer the cod mixture to a bowl. Add the garlic, thyme, paprika, salt, pepper, mustard, coconut aminos and horseradish. Mix together well with clean hands. Add the almond flour and coconut flour and incorporate into the mixture. Lastly, add the eggs and 1 teaspoon of the olive oil, and mix one last time with clean hands.

Form the mixture into 8 balls, and place them 1 inch (2.5 cm) apart on the prepared sheet pan. Gently flatten the balls into ½-inch (1.3-cm)-thick patties with the palm of your hand. Brush the remaining 2 teaspoons (10 ml) of the olive oil over the patties, then bake them for 15 minutes.

Meanwhile, make the sauce: In a high-speed blender, combine the sauce ingredients: first, the roasted red peppers, then the coconut milk, almonds, date, garlic, basil, lemon juice, salt and pepper. Blend until smooth, about 30 seconds.

When the cakes are done baking (they should be firm to the touch), turn the broiler to high and place them 6 inches (15 cm) from the broiler. Broil for 3 to 4 minutes, or until the tops brown. Serve the fish cakes with the sauce on the side and garnish with the scallions, thyme and red pepper flakes, if you'd like.

Prep Time: 10 minutes
Cook Time: 19 minutes
Total Time: 29 minutes
Makes: 8 fish cakes

12 oz (340 g) cod
½ Vidalia onion, chopped
2 cloves garlic, minced
2 tsp (2 g) fresh thyme leaves
¼ tsp paprika
½ tsp salt
¼ tsp freshly ground black pepper
1 tsp prepared brown mustard
1 tsp coconut aminos
½ tsp prepared horseradish
½ cup (50 g) almond flour
2 tbsp (14 g) coconut flour
1 large egg, lightly whisked
1 large egg yolk
1 tbsp (15 ml) olive oil, divided

Roasted Red Pepper Almond Sauce

½ cup (90 g) roasted red peppers, drained
2 tbsp (30 ml) full-fat coconut milk
2 tbsp (12 g) crushed almonds
1 date, pitted and chopped
1 clove garlic, chopped
1 tsp dried basil
1 tsp fresh lemon juice
¼ tsp salt
Pinch of freshly ground black pepper
Chopped scallions, thyme and red pepper flakes, for garnish (optional)

Creamy Tuscan Chicken

Paleo Option / Whole 30 Option / Egg Free / Gluten Free
Dairy Free / Nut Free

This dish was inspired by a creamy Tuscan soup from an upscale Italian restaurant I worked at my summer before college. It is made with bone-in chicken thighs, which are quickly seared and cooked in a creamy tomato and basil broth. My twist is replacing the dairy with coconut milk, which is creamy and pairs well with the other flavors. As in traditional Tuscan cuisine, the tomato and basil are essential here, but this one is ready in much less time, just 30 minutes from start to finish. This meal pairs perfectly with my roasted broccolini (page 75) or over some pasta or rice of choice.

Prep Time: 3 minutes
Cook Time: 27 minutes
Total Time: 30 minutes
Serves: 4

Set the chicken on a plate, pat dry and season with ¼ teaspoon of salt and ⅛ teaspoon of black pepper.

Fill a large saucepan three-quarters full with water and a pinch of salt, and bring to a boil. Cook the pasta according to its package directions, then drain.

Meanwhile, in a large saucepan, heat 2 teaspoons (10 g) of the coconut oil over medium heat and sear the chicken, skin side down, for 3 minutes, then flip and cook for an additional 3 minutes. Transfer to a plate and set aside.

Add the remaining teaspoon of coconut oil, the onion and bell pepper to the saucepan. Sauté for about 3 minutes, or until the onion is soft. Add the garlic and sauté for 30 seconds, or until fragrant. Add the coconut milk, tomatoes, basil, ½ teaspoon of salt, ¼ teaspoon of pepper and the coconut aminos. Bring the sauce to a boil, then lower the heat to medium-low and cook for another 5 minutes.

Add the chicken back to the pot and allow it to simmer until the sauce has thickened and the chicken is cooked through, about 10 minutes.

Serve the pasta and chicken together with cherry tomatoes and fresh basil if you wish.

2 lbs (905 g) bone-in chicken thighs

Salt and freshly ground black pepper

12 oz (340 g) pasta of choice (use veggie noodles for Paleo and Whole 30)

1 tbsp (14 g) coconut oil, divided

½ cup (80 g) diced onion

¼ cup (38 g) seeded and chopped red bell pepper

2 cloves garlic, chopped

1 (13.5-oz [400-ml]) can full-fat coconut milk

¼ cup (45 g) chopped tomatoes

¼ cup (10 g) chopped fresh basil

1 tsp coconut aminos

Cherry tomatoes and fresh basil, for topping

Lamb Curry Meatballs with Avocado Tzatziki

Paleo Option / Whole 30 Option / Gluten Free
Dairy-Free Option / Nut Free

Of all the varieties of red meat, lamb is my favorite to work with. Its distinctive taste requires skill to complement its strong flavor notes. When done right, it becomes a true centerpiece that any meat lover will enjoy. Because of its earthy taste, I find strong spices like curry best smooth out its flavor profile. These meatballs are tender, and the addition of cilantro and mushrooms adds a fresh, light touch, not to mention extra nutrients. They are done in 25 minutes and excellent with an avocado tzatziki.

Preheat the oven to 400°F (200°C). Line a sheet pan with parchment paper, or have ready a large, oven-safe skillet.

Make the meatballs: In a bowl, combine the lamb, egg, onion, mushrooms, cilantro, garlic, curry powder, coconut aminos, salt and pepper, and mix well with clean hands.

Form into balls about 1 inch (2.5 cm) in diameter (you should have about 12 meatballs). Place 1 inch (2.5 cm) apart on the prepared sheet pan (or skillet) and bake for about 18 minutes until the fat has cooked out and meatballs are firm to touch and cooked through.

Meanwhile, make the avocado tzatziki: In a high-speed blender, combine the avocado, garlic and lemon juice and blend until smooth.

Transfer the avocado mixture to a bowl. Add the yogurt, cucumber, dill, mint, coconut aminos, salt and lemon zest, and mix to incorporate. Place the tzatziki in the fridge to chill until ready to serve.

Once the meatballs are ready, remove from the oven, garnish with the dill, red pepper flakes and hemp seeds if you'd like and serve with the tzatziki.

Note: If you prefer another meat, you can substitute 1 pound (455 g) of ground beef or pork for the lamb.

Prep Time: 7 minutes
Cook Time: 18 minutes
Total Time: 25 minutes
Serves: 4

Meatballs

1 lb (455 g) ground lamb

1 large egg

1 medium-sized onion, minced

1 cup (70 g) mushrooms, finely chopped

⅓ cup (13 g) fresh cilantro, chopped

1 clove garlic, minced

2 tsp (4 g) curry powder

2 tsp (10 ml) coconut aminos

½ tsp salt

¼ tsp freshly ground black pepper

Avocado Tzatziki

1 ripe avocado, peeled and pitted

1 clove garlic, chopped

2 tbsp (30 ml) fresh lemon juice

½ cup (115 g) plain Greek yogurt (use dairy-free for Paleo and Whole 30)

3 tbsp (24 g) minced cucumber

1 tbsp (4 g) chopped fresh dill

1 tbsp (3 g) chopped fresh mint

¼ tsp coconut aminos

⅛ tsp salt

¼ tsp lemon zest

For Serving

Fresh dill, red pepper flakes and hemp seeds, for garnish (optional)

Shrimp Bisque

Paleo / Egg Free / Gluten Free / Dairy-Free Option / Nut Free

I have always had a deep affection and appreciation for traditional New England–prepared seafood dishes. In fact, my brother Mike was the head chef of a very popular seafood restaurant in Plymouth, Massachusetts, where he developed an award-winning New England clam chowder. I grew up on rich, decadent, creamy chowder, but sometimes they can be too rich for everyday enjoyment. This bisque can be made totally dairy-free, yet maintains a balance between creamy and brothy with touches of fennel, cumin and tomato. Better yet, you can enjoy this delicacy in just 30 minutes.

Prep Time: 6 minutes
Cook Time: 24 minutes
Total Time: 30 minutes
Serves: 4 to 6

In a small saucepan, combine the shrimp shells, stock and water. Bring to a boil, then lower the heat to medium. Simmer for 5 minutes, then turn off the heat.

Meanwhile, in a medium-sized sauté pan with a lid, heat the butter over medium-high heat. Add the onion and fennel, and sauté for about 4 minutes, or until softened. Add the garlic and sauté for another minute, or until fragrant. Next, add the potatoes and toss everything together.

Add the coconut milk, tomato paste, salt, thyme, hot sauce, coconut aminos, coconut sugar and cumin. Bring the sauce to a boil, then lower the heat to medium-low. Put the lid on the pan.

While the sauce is heating, strain the shrimp broth through a mesh strainer over a bowl in the sink, reserving the liquid; discard the shrimp shells. Remove the lid from the pot of veggies and add the broth to the pot.

Replace the lid and cook for about 10 more minutes, or until the potatoes are soft and can pierce with a fork easily.

Transfer the entire contents of the pot to a high-speed blender and blend until smooth.

Return the bisque to the pan and heat over medium-high heat. Add the shrimp and a squeeze of lemon juice and cook for another 3 minutes, or until they are cooked through.

Serve with fresh tomatoes, scallions and crusty bread, if you'd like.

1 lb (455 g) medium or large shrimp with shells, peeled and deveined, shells reserved

2 cups (475 ml) vegetable or chicken stock

1 cup (240 ml) water

2 tbsp (28 g) unsalted butter, ghee or coconut oil (use oil for dairy-free)

1 medium-sized onion, diced

½ fennel bulb, diced

3 cloves garlic, chopped

3 medium-sized red potatoes, peeled and diced

1 (13.5-oz [400-ml]) can light coconut milk

2 tbsp (32 g) tomato paste

1 tsp salt

½ tsp fresh thyme leaves

A few dashes of hot sauce

3 tbsp (45 ml) coconut aminos

½ tsp coconut sugar

1 tsp ground cumin

Squeeze of fresh lemon juice

Chopped fresh tomatoes, chopped scallions and crusty bread, for serving (optional)

Open-Faced "Stuffed" Peppers

Paleo / Whole 30 / Egg Free / Gluten Free
Dairy-Free Option / Nut Free / Keto

Typical stuffed peppers are filled with rice, ground meat, marinara and cheese. I wanted to create a stuffed pepper that really allowed the protein to shine without too much filling from the rice. My twist on stuffed peppers includes ground veal, which I choose to spend a few extra dollars for on occasion. Veal is slightly leaner than beef and packed with additional nutrients, including selenium. Its strong flavor complements the fresh basil, lemon and currants in this recipe. However, if you prefer ground beef or pork, they also work. I use a method to boil the peppers before baking that allows a delicious and tender stuffed pepper in 30 minutes. It is a Whole 30– and Paleo-friendly meal and can be used as an appetizer if you find smaller-sized peppers.

Prep Time: 4 minutes
Cook Time: 26 minutes
Total Time: 30 minutes
Serves: 4 to 6

Preheat the oven to 375°F (190°C).

Bring a large pot of salted water to a boil, and add the bell peppers. There should be enough water to cover the peppers. Bring back to a boil, cover and cook for 3 minutes.

Meanwhile, in large skillet, heat the ghee over medium-high heat until melted. Add the onion, cabbage and garlic, and sauté until softened, about 4 minutes.

When the peppers are done, remove them from the pot, pat them dry and place them, face down, on a paper towel.

Add the ground veal to the skillet and gently break up the meat, allowing it to sauté and brown with the veggies for about 3 minutes. Add the cherry tomatoes to the skillet, mix together with the veal mixture and cover the pan with a lid or aluminum foil for a minute. Remove the lid, toss and gently press down the tomatoes with a wooden spoon, to allow juices to release.

Add the lemon zest, vinegar, oregano, basil, currants, salt, black pepper and red pepper flakes. Continue to cook until the meat is cooked and everything has combined well, about 4 minutes, continuing to mix gently with a wooden spoon.

Remove the pan from the heat. Place the bell pepper halves, cut side up, in a casserole dish. Drizzle them with olive oil and sprinkle with a little salt and pepper. Fill each half with the meat mixture, slightly overfilling the bell pepper halves. Bake on the bottom rack for 10 minutes until the peppers are heated throughout. Garnish with the parsley and serve with the lemon wedges on the side, if you wish.

3 bell peppers, seeded and sliced down the middle into halves

1 tbsp (14 g) ghee or coconut oil (use oil for dairy-free)

1 medium-sized onion, diced

1 cup (90 g) finely chopped cabbage

3 cloves garlic, chopped

1 lb (455 g) ground veal

1 heaping cup (170 g) cherry tomatoes

½ tsp lemon zest

1 tbsp (15 ml) balsamic vinegar

½ tsp dried oregano

2 to 3 tbsp (5 to 7 g) chopped fresh basil

2 tbsp (19 g) dried currants

1 tsp salt, plus more for sprinkling

¼ tsp freshly ground black pepper, plus more for sprinkling

¼ tsp red pepper flakes

Olive oil, for drizzling

Chopped fresh parsley and lemon wedges, for serving (optional)

Mango and Pineapple Chipotle Chicken

Paleo / Whole 30 Option / Egg Free / Gluten Free / Dairy Free / Nut Free

The special element to this dish is the sauce. Boneless, skinless chicken thighs have the ability to truly absorb the mango and pineapple flavors while maintaining a tender and juicy inside. I intentionally created this marinade to have a thicker consistency so that the chicken would not have to marinate too long, but instead, they have a sweet and spicy coating, almost like a chicken wing does. The chicken cooks in the oven in just 22 minutes, making it easy for any night of the week. I like to serve this meal with a group of friends, because it can become a customizable taco spread or just a delicious protein served on its own over salad.

Prep Time: 8 minutes
Cook Time: 22 minutes
Total Time: 30 minutes
Serves: 6 to 8

Preheat the oven to 450°F (230°C). Place a wire rack over a sheet pan lined with parchment paper. Set aside.

In a high-speed blender, combine the mango, pineapple juice, onion, garlic, honey, coconut milk, lime juice, chipotle chile powder, cumin, tomato paste, salt and paprika, and blend until smooth. Stir the cilantro into the sauce.

Place the chicken in a large bowl, then pour the sauce over the chicken and toss.

Place the chicken on the rack over the sheet pan, leaving 1 inch (2.5 cm) or so between each thigh. Spoon on half of the sauce in the bowl to coat the chicken well (the sauce should be thick enough). Discard the remaining sauce. Drizzle the olive oil over the chicken.

Bake for 20 to 22 minutes, or until the internal temperature reaches 165°F (73°C). Serve with tortillas, mango, jalapeños, tomatoes, cabbage, scallions, avocado and salsa (if using).

½ ripe mango, peeled, pitted and chopped

½ cup (120 ml) pure pineapple juice

½ medium-sized onion, chopped

2 cloves garlic, chopped

1 tbsp (15 ml) honey or date syrup (use date syrup for Whole 30)

2 tbsp (30 ml) full-fat coconut milk

1 tbsp (15 ml) fresh lime juice

1½ tsp (4 g) chipotle chile powder

1 tsp ground cumin

1 tsp tomato paste

½ tsp salt

¼ tsp paprika

1 tbsp (3 g) chopped fresh cilantro

2 lbs (905 g) boneless, skinless chicken thighs

2 tsp (10 ml) olive oil, for drizzling

Paleo tortillas (omit for Whole 30), fresh sliced mango, sliced jalapeño peppers, chopped tomatoes, chopped cabbage, chopped scallions, avocado and salsa, for serving (optional)

Comforting
FOODS ON THE GO

The warm, pungent aroma of chili powder and cumin infusing the air soon filled the entire old apartment building. The gigantic simmering black pot took up half of my tiny little stovetop. "The boys" always seemed to roll in right on time for kickoff, usually straight out of bed, and probably having only gone to sleep a few hours earlier. I mean, it was Sunday after all, the day after Saturday, and we were college kids in our junior year . . . enough said. I'd usually send one of them to the store to grab some chips and whatever fixings they wanted to top off the chili. I had a studio apartment; my kitchen and dining room were filled with friends. It was small, always a bit crowded, but it was comfortable, cozy and felt like home. I always felt a bit homesick on Sundays, missing football day spreads and cozy evening dinners. So, I learned to adapt our family festivities with my friends—my way.

It was that time, my junior year of college, when I really began to focus on a more whole foods–centric diet. The first couple of years, like most college kids, I lived on food that was quick and easy. Pizza and burrito deliveries became my go-tos, since I didn't cook as much while I tried to adjust to my new life away from home. I moved into that little studio apartment with that tiny stove and limited amount of counter space, but it was all mine and

I made the most of it. I began learning more about a holistic, whole food approach to eating. In that kitchen was where I began experimenting with cooking foods that were more nutritionally dense and energizing. My closest friends were very picky college-aged guys, so I quickly learned to adapt my whole foods approach to making versions of classic "comfort foods" that they would actually try. In that kitchen, I developed my spin-off of my mother's classic chili.

You'll find in this chapter all the classic dishes that I find comforting, the ones that make my soul feel better when I'm having a tough day. I've said it before, but food does hold so much power. Some days, a warm bowl of chili is all I need to bring me right back to watching a football game with my entire family cozied up next to my dogs. Of course, you'll find that Hearty Real Food Chili (page 59) in this chapter, along with my crunchy Cashew-Crusted Chicken Tenders (page 52). Plus, I'll even teach you how to create a mouthwatering pizza (page 44) in less time than it would take for delivery to arrive, using a crust made from nutrient-dense sweet potatoes. If classic comfort foods bring you joy, I guarantee you'll find comfort here.

Classic Burger and Sweet Potato Fries Sheet Pan

Paleo Option / Whole 30 Option / Gluten-Free Option
Dairy Free / Nut Free

Who can relate to craving a juicy burger with a side of crispy fries? In 30 minutes, using my parboiled method, you can cook both the burger and fries together in the oven. My own burger twist: I find adding my favorite toppings *into* the burger, instead of on top, increases the flavor and moisture to prevent the burger from overcooking. This allows you to make the best combo burger and fries while using just one sheet pan.

Prep Time: 10 minutes
Cook Time: 20 minutes
Total Time: 30 minutes
Serves: 4 to 6

Preheat the oven to 425°F (220°C). Line a sheet pan with parchment paper. Line half of the sheet pan with a piece of aluminum foil (on top of the parchment paper), covering the length and only half the width of the pan.

Parboil the sweet potatoes: Bring a pot of water with a little salt to a boil. Add the sweet potatoes and boil, uncovered, for 2 minutes. Remove from the pot, pat dry and set aside.

Meanwhile, make the burgers: In a large bowl, combine the beef, mushrooms, onion, salt, pepper, garlic powder, coconut aminos and egg. Using clean hands, mix together until all the ingredients are incorporated. Form the mixture into 6 small patties. Place them in a single layer on the parchment side of the sheet pan.

In a small bowl, mix together the salt, onion powder, thyme and paprika. Toss the sweet potatoes with enough olive oil to coat the outside, plus the spice mixture. Arrange the fries in a single layer on the foil, then place the sheet pan on the bottom rack of the oven. Bake for 16 minutes, flipping both the burgers and fries after about 8 minutes.

Remove the sheet pan from the oven, and transfer the burgers to a plate. Turn the broiler to high and place the sheet pan of fries 6 inches (15 cm) from the broiler. Broil for 1 to 2 minutes per side, or until crispy. Serve the burgers with the buns and toppings of your choice and the fries on the side.

Sweet Potatoes

1 lb (455 g) sweet potatoes, cut into fries

½ tsp salt

½ tsp onion powder

½ tsp dried thyme

¼ tsp paprika

Olive oil

Burgers

1 lb (455 g) ground beef

1 cup (70 g) minced mushrooms

⅔ cup (110 g) finely minced onion

½ tsp salt

¼ tsp freshly ground black pepper

¼ tsp garlic powder

2 tsp (10 ml) coconut aminos

1 large egg

For Serving (optional)

Burger buns (omit for Paleo and Whole 30, gluten-free if needed)

Lettuce

Sliced tomatoes

Shredded cabbage

Sliced pineapple

Mashed avocado

Nourishing Sweet Potato Pizza

Paleo Option / Gluten Free / Dairy-Free Option / Nut-Free Option

Pizza, the ultimate comfort food. Just hearing the name alone immediately brings me a sense of satisfaction. There are so many variations, I honestly don't think I could choose just one favorite. A good gluten-free pizza crust was one recipe I set out to create after going gluten-free. My crust is made with sweet potato, requires no yeast and comes together in less time than you'd spend waiting for the delivery to arrive. Choose your desired toppings; my favorites are pesto, fresh or dairy-free mozzarella, fresh tomatoes and greens. Did I mention the crust is also Paleo-friendly?

Prep Time: 9 minutes
Cook Time: 21 minutes
Total Time: 30 minutes
Serves: 4

Preheat the oven to 400°F (200°C). Line a sheet pan with parchment paper.

In a medium-sized bowl, stir together the cassava flour, tapioca flour, coconut flour, baking powder, oregano and salt, and set aside.

Add the baked sweet potatoes, olive oil and eggs to a high-speed blender, and blend until smooth. Scrape the sweet potato mixture into the flour mixture. Using a fork, fold together until a sticky dough forms.

Spread the dough on the prepared sheet pan, using an oiled rubber spatula. Spread evenly to about ¼ inch (6 mm) thick, into the shape of your choice (I like making a rectangle).

Bake on the bottom rack for 14 minutes. Remove from the oven and increase the heat to 425°F (220°C).

Add the toppings of your choice. If using my suggested toppings, spread the pesto on the pizza, then top with the mozzarella, tomatoes and basil. Place the pizza back in the oven directly on the rack (remove the sheet pan at this point). Bake for another 5 to 7 minutes until the cheese has melted and the edges of the crust are dry. Top with fresh arugula, black pepper and red pepper flakes. Follow this procedure if you add your own preferred toppings.

Note: This recipe uses pre-baked sweet potatoes. To bake, preheat the oven to 400°F (200°C), pierce each side of the potatoes twice, then wrap them in aluminum foil and bake for 45 minutes, until tender. Alternatively, you could cut the potatoes into cubes, add them to boiling water and cook for 5 to 7 minutes, until tender.

1 cup (128 g) cassava flour

¼ cup (42 g) tapioca flour

¼ cup (28 g) coconut flour

1 tsp baking powder

1 tsp dried oregano

1 tsp salt

2 medium-sized sweet potatoes (about 5.5 oz [150 g] total raw weight), washed and baked (see Note)

2 tbsp (30 ml) olive oil, plus more for spatula

2 large eggs

Toppings (or use the toppings of your choice)

½ cup (130 g) prepared pesto (dairy-free, if needed)

8 oz (225 g) fresh mozzarella cheese, sliced (dairy-free and nut-free, if needed)

2 medium-sized tomatoes, sliced

¼ cup (10 g) fresh torn basil leaves

⅓ cup (7 g) fresh arugula

¼ tsp freshly ground black pepper

Pinch of red pepper flakes

Dairy-Free Classic Mac and Cheese

Egg Free / Gluten Free / Dairy Free / Vegan

My mom rarely made macaroni and cheese when I was growing up. When she did, she used Velveeta cheese, one of the only times my mom would use processed food. As much as I loved a rich real-deal creamy mac and cheese, it always seemed to leave me feeling weighed down. When I developed this recipe, I set out to duplicate the Velveeta cheese texture. After much experimentation, I found a winner. Using cashew butter, miso, potato starch and tapioca flour, I was able to re-create that same cheesy goodness without the dairy. Bonus: It takes only 15 minutes. This is one even picky kids would enjoy.

Prep Time: 5 minutes
Cook Time: 10 minutes
Total Time: 15 minutes
Serves: 4

In a small saucepan, bring 1 cup (240 ml) of water to a boil. Add the carrot and boil until tender, 5 to 7 minutes.

Meanwhile, in a high-speed blender, combine the oat milk, water, cashew butter, olive oil, potato starch, tapioca flour, coconut aminos, salt, miso, vinegar, mustard powder, garlic powder and onion powder. Blend until smooth.

Once the carrot is done cooking, drain and transfer to the mixture in the blender. Blend again. Transfer the sauce to a small saucepan.

Heat over medium heat, whisking, until the sauce thickens. This should take about 3 minutes.

Pour the sauce over the cooked pasta. Serve with some steamed broccolini and garnish with the hemp seeds if you'd like.

1 large carrot, chopped

¼ cup (60 ml) oat milk (or any plain unsweetened dairy-free milk)

5 tbsp (75 ml) water

2 tbsp (32 g) cashew butter

1 tbsp (15 ml) olive oil

1 tbsp (9 g) potato starch

1½ tsp (4 g) tapioca flour

1 tsp coconut aminos

¾ tsp salt

½ tsp white miso paste

½ tsp apple cider vinegar

½ tsp mustard powder

¼ tsp garlic powder

¼ tsp onion powder

1 lb (455 g) dried pasta of choice, cooked according to package instructions

Steamed broccolini, for serving (optional)

Hemp seeds, for garnish (optional)

Mediterranean Turkey Burgers

Gluten Free / Nut Free

I spent one summer nannying for a family in the evenings. More often than not, I would be cooking myself dinner at their home, and I would often leave extra for them to enjoy. This burger was one of the first meals I left behind and it was an instant hit, resulting in a position as a personal chef. As with all my burgers and meatballs, I bake them, which means 5 minutes of prep and they are in the oven. They are filled with dill, lemon, feta and hidden veggies. This Greek-inspired burger is light, fresh and a very satisfying twist to the standard American fare.

Prep Time: 5 minutes
Cook Time: 22 minutes
Total Time: 27 minutes
Makes: 8 patties

Preheat the oven to 400°F (200°C).

In a medium-sized bowl, combine all the burger ingredients: turkey, cauliflower rice, egg, red onion, feta cheese, red peppers, dill, oregano, salt and pepper. With clean hands, mix well together to incorporate.

Form the mixture into small patties ¾ inch (2 cm) thick (about eight patties) and place them 1 inch (2.5 cm) apart on a dry sheet pan. Brush the tops of the patties with some olive oil.

Bake the patties for 20 to 22 minutes until cooked through. They should be firm to the touch. Remove them from the oven when they are done. Serve with some chopped olives, chopped tomatoes, more feta, red onion slices and lemon wedges if you wish.

1 lb (455 g) turkey (93% lean)

1 cup (100 g) fresh or frozen cauliflower rice

1 large egg

¾ cup (120 g) finely minced red onion

½ cup (75 g) crumbled feta cheese

¼ cup (45 g) chopped roasted red peppers

2 tbsp (8 g) chopped fresh dill

1½ tsp (2 g) dried oregano

½ tsp salt

¼ tsp freshly ground black pepper

Olive oil, for brushing

Lemon wedges, for serving (optional)

Optional Toppings

Chopped olives

Chopped tomatoes

Feta cheese

Red onion slices

My Classic Pasta Marinara

Paleo / Whole 30 / Gluten Free / Dairy-Free Option
Nut Free / Vegan Option

Everyone has their preference, but for me, a lighter sauce wins every time. What also makes my marinara special is that it is packed with hidden veggies. When making a classic tomato sauce, you need to balance out the acidity. I choose to do so with a combination of zucchini and carrots. These veggies add a slight sweetness without adding sugar. Everyone is always amazed that this recipe yields the flavor of a sauce that has been cooking all day, but it takes just 30 minutes. Serve it over your favorite pasta or Paleo-friendly spaghetti squash. Make sure to freeze any extra in ready-to-go portions for busy nights.

Prep Time: 5 minutes
Cook Time: 25 minutes
Total Time: 30 minutes
Makes: 6 large servings of sauce

In a large saucepan, heat the olive oil over medium-high heat.

Add the onion, mushrooms, carrot and zucchini. Sauté for about 4 minutes, or until softened. Add the garlic and sauté for another minute. Add the salt, pepper, oregano and coconut aminos and stir into the veggie mixture. Add the tomatoes, broth, basil and hot sauce.

Bring the sauce to a boil, then lower the heat to medium. Let simmer for 20 minutes, stirring occasionally. Then, turn off the heat, and stir in the parsley and butter.

Serve the sauce over your pasta or veggie pasta of choice and top with cherry tomatoes, Parmesan and basil if you wish.

1 tbsp (15 ml) olive oil

1 medium-sized onion, finely chopped

1 cup (70 g) minced mushrooms

1 cup (110 g) finely shredded carrot

1 cup (120 g) finely shredded zucchini

2 tsp (6 g) minced garlic

1 tsp salt

¼ tsp freshly ground black pepper

2 tsp (2 g) dried oregano

2 tbsp (30 ml) coconut aminos

1 (28-oz [800-g]) can crushed tomatoes

1½ cups (355 ml) bone broth (sub veggie stock for vegan)

½ cup (20 g) chopped fresh basil

A few dashes of hot sauce

2 tbsp (8 g) chopped fresh parsley

1 tbsp (14 g) unsalted butter or ghee (sub vegan butter for vegan or dairy-free)

Cooked pasta or veggie pasta of choice, for serving

Fresh cherry tomatoes, Parmesan cheese and fresh basil, for topping (optional)

Cashew-Crusted Chicken Tenders

Paleo / Whole 30 / Gluten Free / Dairy Free / Keto

These Whole 30– and Paleo-friendly chicken tenders are crunchy on the outside, just as you want them to be. The coating of ground cashews adds a nutty dimension and buttery richness without the butter. You can air fry them or bake in the oven—either method gives great results. Served with my plantain fries (page 127) and some broccolini, you will have all your bases covered.

Prep Time: 10 minutes
Cook Time: 10 minutes
(using an air fryer)
Total Time: 20 minutes
Serves: 4

Preheat either an air fryer to 375°F (190°C) or a conventional oven to 400°F (200°C).

In a high-speed blender, combine the cashews, coconut flour, salt, paprika, garlic powder, onion powder and chipotle chile powder. Blend until the cashews are crumbly but not powdery.

Transfer the cashew mixture to a shallow bowl, and place the whisked egg in a separate shallow bowl.

Dip the tenders into the whisked egg and then into the crumb mixture.

Spray the tenders lightly with oil. Air fry for 9 to 10 minutes, or bake in the oven on a sheet pan for 15 to 20 minutes, or until the internal temperature reaches 165°F (73°C), flipping at about the 5-minute point for the air fryer or the 8-minute point for the conventional oven. Serve with the chopped chives, hemp seeds, avocado, strawberries and ketchup if you wish.

½ cup (70 g) raw, unsalted cashews
2 tbsp (14 g) coconut flour
¼ tsp salt
¼ tsp paprika
¼ tsp garlic powder
¼ tsp onion powder
¼ tsp chipotle chile powder
1 large egg, whisked
1 lb (455 g) chicken tenders
Cooking oil spray

For Serving (optional)
Chopped chives
Hemp seeds
Avocado slices
Strawberries
Ketchup

Sweet-and-Spicy Sticky Chicken Drumsticks

Who doesn't love a good sticky wing sauce? This is one of my favorite quick and budget-friendly weeknight meals. Chicken drumsticks are inexpensive and easy to cook. The sauce, sweetened with date syrup, comes together in 5 minutes on the stovetop. It has a touch of sweetness, balanced with a hint of heat and undertones of garlic flavor. Using the air-fryer method produces a crispy exterior and a juicy wing with minimal oil in just 25 minutes. In case you don't own an air fryer, I have included directions for cooking these in a conventional oven, but note that the cook time will be longer. Pair these with a zoodle salad in the summer.

Prep Time: 5 minutes
Cook Time: 20 minutes (using an air fryer)
Total Time: 25 minutes
Serves: 4

To air fry: Preheat an air fryer to 400°F (200°C). Place the chicken in the air fryer and drizzle olive oil over the chicken. Air fry for 10 minutes, flip and air fry for 10 more minutes.

To bake in a conventional oven: Preheat the oven to 425°F (220°C). Line a sheet pan with parchment paper. Place the chicken on the prepared pan, drizzle with olive oil and bake for 35 to 45 minutes until the internal temperature reaches 165°F (73°C).

Meanwhile, make the sauce: In a medium-sized bowl, whisk together the lime juice, coconut aminos, date syrup, fish sauce, sriracha, garlic, cilantro and sesame oil.

Transfer the mixture to a small saucepan and bring to a boil. Then, lower the heat to medium-low and cook for about 5 minutes, whisking every minute or so. Remove from the heat.

When the chicken is done cooking, brush the sauce all over or toss the drumsticks with the sauce in a bowl. Garnish with the sesame seeds and scallions, if you wish.

2 lbs (905 g) chicken drumsticks, patted dry and seasoned with salt and pepper

Olive oil

Sauce

3 tbsp (45 ml) fresh lime juice

2 tbsp (30 ml) coconut aminos

1 tbsp (15 ml) date syrup or honey (use date syrup for Whole 30)

1 tsp Asian fish sauce (Red Boat brand is Paleo and Whole 30)

1 tsp sriracha

1 tsp minced garlic

1 tbsp (3 g) minced fresh cilantro

1 tsp sesame oil

Sesame seeds and chopped scallions, for garnish (optional)

Creamy Pumpkin–Sweet Potato Curried Soup

Paleo / Whole 30 Option / Gluten Free / Dairy-Free Option / Nut Free Vegan Option

One brisk fall afternoon, staring at a half can of pumpkin puree, I thought, "What can I do with this?" I decided to make my first soup of the season. Always ready to experiment, I glanced over to my special curry spice blend and started putting it all together. I grabbed a sweet potato and a can of coconut milk and started cooking. Twenty-five minutes later, I pureed my concoction in the blender. Seriously, the best soup I ever made. Most of the cooking time here is hands-off, so it's a great one to throw on the stove without much work at all. Special note: My Homemade Curry Powder is a necessity and key to this recipe and should not be replaced with other curry powders.

Make the curry powder: In a small bowl, combine the coriander, cumin, turmeric, ginger, mustard powder, chipotle chile powder and black pepper. Mix together with a fork, making sure all the spices are evenly blended. Set aside 1½ teaspoons (3 g) to use in this recipe; you will have extra to use at another time (store in an airtight jar).

Make the soup: In a large soup pot, heat the olive oil over medium-high heat until sizzling. Add the onion, celery and garlic. Sauté for 2 to 3 minutes, until softened. Add the coconut milk, stock, pumpkin, sweet potato, maple syrup, paprika, the 1½ teaspoons (3 g) of homemade curry powder, salt and coconut aminos, and bring to a boil.

Mix together with a wooden spoon. Cover, lower the heat to low and let cook for about 20 minutes, or until the sweet potato is tender enough to be pierced with a fork.

Transfer the soup to a high-speed blender and blend until very smooth, like a puree. Stir in the butter (if using). Serve immediately with the toppings of your choice.

Prep Time: 5 minutes
Cook Time: 25 minutes
Total Time: 30 minutes
Serves: 4 to 6

Homemade Curry Powder

2 tbsp (12 g) ground coriander

2 tbsp (14 g) ground cumin

1½ tbsp (10 g) ground turmeric

2 tsp (4 g) ground ginger

1 tsp mustard powder

½ tsp chipotle chile powder

½ tsp freshly ground black pepper

1 tbsp (15 ml) olive oil

½ medium-sized onion, chopped

2 celery ribs, chopped

2 cloves garlic, chopped

1 (13.5-oz [400-ml]) can full-fat coconut milk, plus more for garnish

1⅔ cups (400 ml) stock of choice

½ (15-oz [425-g]) can pure pumpkin puree

1 medium-sized sweet potato, peeled and cut into ½" (1.3-cm) chunks

1 tbsp (15 ml) pure maple syrup (omit for Whole 30)

2 tsp (5 g) paprika

1½ tsp (9 g) salt

1 tsp coconut aminos

1 to 2 tbsp (14 to 28 g) unsalted butter, ghee or coconut oil (optional)

Pepitas, almonds and cilantro (optional)

Hearty Real Food Chili

Paleo Option / Whole 30 Option / Egg Free / Gluten Free / Dairy-Free Option / Nut Free

While I was growing up, football Sundays meant a great pot of chili. Being from New England meant making the playoffs, which meant more chili . . . win-win. My recipe is adapted from my mother's chili. What makes mine different from most chili recipes is that I use no beans, making it Paleo-friendly, plus in 30 minutes you have a chili that tastes as if it's been on the stove all day. I packed it with extra veggies to simulate that chunky, hearty nature associated with classic chili. I prefer to use ground turkey because I find it absorbs flavor better and does not overpower the seasonings in the chili. If you prefer beef, by all means substitute.

Prep Time: 7 minutes
Cook Time: 23 minutes
Ready Time: 30 minutes
Serves: 4 to 6

In a medium-sized saucepan, heat the olive oil over medium-high heat.

Add the onion, celery, carrots and mushrooms, and sauté for 3 to 4 minutes, or until the onion is soft. Add the garlic and sauté for another 30 seconds, or until fragrant. Add the ground turkey and sauté for about 3 minutes, or until browned. Add the tomatoes, stock, cumin, oregano, paprika, chile powder, honey and salt. Mix everything together with a wooden spoon.

Bring the mixture to a boil, then lower the heat and simmer for at least 15 minutes. Stir in the cilantro and hot sauce (if using). Serve with any of the toppings that you'd like.

1 tbsp (15 ml) olive oil

1 medium-sized onion, chopped

2 celery ribs, chopped

2 large carrots, chopped

½ cup (35 g) chopped mushrooms

1 tsp garlic, minced

1 lb (455 g) ground turkey (93% lean)

1½ cups (366 g) crushed tomatoes

1 cup (240 ml) chicken stock, chicken bone broth or veggie stock

1 tbsp (7 g) ground cumin

1 tsp dried oregano

½ tsp paprika

1 tsp chipotle chile powder or regular chili powder

1 tsp honey (omit for Whole 30)

½ tsp salt, or more to taste

¼ cup (10 g) chopped fresh cilantro (optional)

A few dashes of hot sauce (optional)

Optional Toppings

Plain Greek yogurt or sour cream (omit or use dairy-free, if needed)

Chopped avocado

Chopped tomatoes

Sliced scallions

Shredded cheese (omit or use dairy-free, if needed)

White Chicken Chili Soup

Egg Free / Gluten Free / Dairy-Free Option / Nut Free

This twist on chili can be enjoyed year-round. This recipe is fresh in flavor due to the lime juice and cilantro. This recipe comes together in just 30 minutes. I use boneless, skinless chicken thighs, which cook quickly and retain the moisture when cooked in stock. Adding white beans creates a buttery undertone and thickens the broth perfectly. My secret ingredient is cumin, which as a bonus stimulates better digestion. Crumble some tortilla chips on top and you will not be disappointed.

Prep Time: 10 minutes
Cook Time: 20 minutes
Total Time: 30 minutes
Serves: 4 to 6

In a large saucepan, heat the ghee over medium heat. Once hot, add the onion and carrots, and sauté for 3 to 4 minutes, or until the onion is soft. Add the garlic and sauté for another 30 seconds, or until the garlic is fragrant.

Add the broth, lime juice, coconut aminos, cilantro, oregano, cumin, salt and jalapeño, and cook for 5 minutes.

Add the beans and chicken thighs and bring back to a boil, then lower the heat to medium, cover and cook for another 10 minutes.

Remove the chicken and place it on a plate. Shred the chicken with a fork and add the chicken back to the soup.

Serve the soup warm with any of the toppings that you'd like.

1 tbsp (14 g) ghee or coconut oil, or (15 ml) olive oil (use coconut or olive oil for dairy-free)

1½ cups (240 g) chopped Vidalia onion

3 large carrots, quartered and then chopped

3 cloves garlic, minced

4 cups (960 ml) chicken bone broth, veggie stock or prepared bouillon

2 tbsp (30 ml) fresh lime juice

2 tbsp (30 ml) coconut aminos

¼ cup (10 g) fresh cilantro, chopped

1½ tbsp (6 g) fresh oregano, or 2 tsp (2 g) dried

1½ tbsp (10 g) ground cumin

¼ to ½ tsp salt or more, to taste (if using a higher-sodium stock, start with ¼ tsp and add to taste)

1 tsp minced fresh jalapeño pepper

1 (14-oz [400-g]) can cannellini beans, drained and rinsed

1½ lbs (680 g) boneless, skinless chicken thighs

Optional Toppings

Tortilla chips

Fresh cilantro

Chopped jalapeño pepper

Peeled, pitted and chopped avocado

Chopped tomatoes

Hemp seeds

Veggies
TO FUEL YOUR BODY

I opened the cooler to find a big stack of my mom's famous hummus and tabbouleh sandwiches. Creamy garlic and herb hummus smothered on one side of the bread, a slice of crisp romaine lettuce, the middle stacked with whatever leftover veggies we had in the fridge and her famous tabbouleh on the other side. Just thinking about it makes my mouth water. They were always perfectly wrapped in parchment paper and plastic wrap, so you never lost a bite of that delicious filling. It didn't matter how old I was—if it was a beach day, my mom packed sandwiches for everyone. With the sun beating down on my skin and smells of sunscreen and salty ocean water filling the air, I sat down in my chair, unwrapped my sandwich and smiled contentedly with each bite.

I was never a picky eater as a child. My parents had introduced us to a wide variety of foods at such a young age—in fact, I had my first oyster at two years old. It was a blessing to have experienced meals that were home cooked and well prepared. This included veggies. I was never told to "eat my veggies," because my mom had a way with making vegetables their own delicacy. We always had at least one veggie side at dinner. Sometimes she whipped up something more indulgent, such as her cauliflower au gratin, but most of the time, they were

simply prepared. It was my mother who taught me that a little bit of spice and herbs are necessary to make a seemingly bland vegetable taste delicious on its own—a lesson I follow to this day. I discovered throughout the years that vegetables are my favorite foods to prepare. They are versatile, and I like to sneak them into recipes for extra texture, flavor and nutrients. However, there is so much you can do with them on their own, with a little creativity.

In this chapter, I'm sharing with you an assortment of easy recipes that bring basic veggies to a whole new level. I took that original recipe of tabbouleh from my mom to create a new twist, using cauliflower rice instead of grains to create my Stuffed Zucchini with Cauliflower Tabbouleh (page 67). These are always fun to eat and beautiful to serve to guests. If you're a cauliflower fan like me, I have also included my Addictive Za'atar Roasted Cauliflower Bites with Tahini (page 72), whose dip you'll want to pour over everything. Don't feel like cooking? I got you! You'll find three of my go-to salads (pages 79, 80 and 83) that are far from boring. The best part? These are all done with very little time and effort.

Stuffed Zucchini with Cauliflower Tabbouleh

Paleo / Whole 30 / Egg Free / Gluten Free / Dairy Free / Nut Free / Vegan

This dish is reminiscent of one of my favorite starchy sides as a child, but I replaced the grains with two of my favorite veggies: cauliflower and zucchini. Simply roast the zucchini boats and then use cauliflower rice to create the tabbouleh. It has traditional Middle Eastern flair, but it's made with 100 percent veggies and olive oil. This 30-minute dish makes a great side or you can top with a protein for a full meal.

Prep Time: 10 minutes
Cook Time: 20 minutes
Total Time: 30 minutes
Makes: 10 large or 16 small zucchini halves

Preheat the oven to 425°F (220°C).

Make the zucchini: Using a spoon, scoop out the zucchini flesh, leaving about a ¼-inch (6-mm) margin all around; set aside. Discard the flesh or save it to add to an egg scramble or salads. Place the hollowed-out zucchini on a plate, drizzle with the olive oil and season with salt and pepper. Transfer them directly onto an oven rack, hollow side up, for 20 minutes, or until tender.

Meanwhile, make the tabbouleh: In a medium-sized saucepan, combine the cauliflower rice and water. Bring to a boil, stir and then cook for 2 minutes.

Place the ice in a bowl. Pour the cauliflower rice into a mesh strainer or mesh bag placed over the bowl of ice, making sure it is touching the ice. Allow it to sit for 10 minutes to cool.

In a large bowl, combine the tomatoes, cucumber, scallions, parsley, mint (if using), salt and red pepper flakes and toss together. Add the olive oil, lemon juice and coconut aminos. Mix them in, using a spoon. Set the bowl aside.

Remove the cauliflower from the ice, and squeeze as much liquid as possible out of the cauliflower. Add the cauliflower to the tomato mixture and mix to combine.

Remove the zucchini from the oven and set them, hollow side up, on a large plate.

Divide the tabbouleh among the zucchini halves, about a heaping ⅓ cup (37 g) of the tabbouleh into each zucchini half.

Zucchini

5 medium-sized or 8 small zucchini, halved

1 tbsp (15 ml) olive oil

½ tsp salt

¼ tsp freshly ground black pepper

Tabbouleh

4 cups (400 g) frozen cauliflower rice, thawed

1 cup (240 ml) water

6 cups (840 g) ice

1 cup (150 g) diced cherry tomatoes

½ English cucumber, washed and finely chopped

2 scallions, finely chopped

1 bunch parsley, washed, dried and finely chopped

2 tbsp (5 g) finely chopped fresh mint (optional, but recommended)

½ tsp salt

¼ tsp red pepper flakes

2 tbsp (30 ml) olive oil

2 tbsp (30 ml) fresh lemon juice

1 tsp coconut aminos

Garlic-Miso Balsamic Roasted Mushrooms

Egg Free / Gluten Free / Dairy-Free Option / Nut Free / Vegan

Influenced by my grandfather, who spent a fair amount of time in Japan and other parts of Eastern Asia, I've always enjoyed authentic Asian flavors with a particular interest in miso. Miso, made typically from soybeans, is a fermented paste that is earthy, salty and has a touch of sweetness. I chose to showcase mushrooms in this glaze due to their high compatibility with almost any combination of foods. They cook quickly in under 30 minutes. I added balsamic vinegar, a slightly sweet component, to balance out the salty, earthy tone of miso, creating a perfect glaze. I enjoy these as a side with simple proteins or served as an appetizer for group settings.

Prep Time: 10 minutes
Cook Time: 17 minutes
Total Time: 27 minutes
Serves: 4

Preheat the oven to 400°F (200°C).

In a small bowl, whisk together the coconut aminos, vinegar, miso and sriracha. Set aside.

Trim the stems of the mushrooms and wipe with a damp paper towel to remove any dirt or debris.

In a cast-iron or oven-safe skillet, melt the butter over medium-high heat. Add the mushrooms and garlic, toss them to coat with the butter, then turn off the heat. Add the miso mixture and toss, using a rubber spatula or wooden spoon, and make sure everything is coated. Arrange the mushrooms in the skillet into a single layer and turn them stem side down.

Place the skillet on the bottom rack of the oven. Bake the mushrooms for 15 minutes, flipping once at about the 8-minute point.

Remove the mushrooms from the oven, and top them with scallions and cilantro (if using).

2 tbsp (30 ml) coconut aminos

2 tbsp (30 ml) balsamic vinegar

1 tbsp (16 g) white miso paste

Dash of sriracha

1 lb (455 g) baby bella or white mushrooms

1 tbsp (14 g) unsalted butter, ghee or coconut oil (use oil for dairy-free)

2 cloves garlic, minced

Chopped scallions, for garnish (optional)

Chopped fresh cilantro, for garnish (optional)

Smashed Brussels Sprouts with Maple-Mustard Apples

Paleo / Egg Free / Gluten Free / Dairy Free / Nut Free / Vegan

This is a great holiday recipe that is also suitable for everyday eats: apples and maple syrup for sweetness, capers for salt and mustard for an added pop. To ensure tender yet crisp, vibrant Brussels, quickly blanch them then broil them. This will accelerate the cooking time, making this one done in 25 minutes. If you prefer bacon over capers, crush some cooked bacon into the apple mixture for that salty component.

Prep Time: 10 minutes
Cook Time: 15 minutes
Total Time: 25 minutes
Serves: 4

Set the oven to broil on high.

Make the Brussels sprouts: In a medium-sized saucepan, combine 4 cups (960 ml) of water with a pinch of salt and bring to a boil. Add the Brussels sprouts to the water and cover, then cook for about 4 minutes. They should be slightly tender but not soft.

Meanwhile, make the topping: In a small bowl, combine the apple, mustard, maple syrup, vinegar, olive oil and capers and mix together. Set aside.

When the Brussels sprouts are done, drain the water and place them on a paper towel. Pat them dry.

Using the flat bottom of a cup or mug, smash the Brussels sprouts so they are slightly flattened. Place them in a bowl, toss with the olive oil, salt and pepper, transfer them to a sheet pan and spread them out evenly. Place the sheet pan 8 inches (20 cm) from the broiler and broil for 3 minutes, until the tops crisp. Remove the sheet pan from the oven and flip them over, making sure they are all flipped with the crisp side down. Broil for another 1½ to 2 minutes, until the second side is crisp. Remove from the oven, and transfer them to a bowl. Watch them carefully as they broil. They will crisp quickly.

Spoon the apple mixture over the Brussels sprouts. Toss and serve.

Brussels Sprouts

½ tsp salt, plus a pinch for cooking water

1 lb (455 g) Brussels sprouts, trimmed

2 tbsp (30 ml) olive oil

¼ tsp freshly ground black pepper

Maple-Mustard Apple Topping

⅔ cup (75 g) diced apple (a sweet variety such as Fuji, Pink Lady or Gala works best)

1 tbsp (11 g) prepared spicy brown or Dijon mustard

1 tbsp (15 ml) pure maple syrup

2 tsp (10 ml) apple cider vinegar

2 tsp (10 ml) olive oil

1 tsp capers, drained and minced

Addictive Za'atar Roasted Cauliflower Bites with Tahini

Paleo / Whole 30 / Egg Free / Gluten Free / Dairy Free / Vegan

This vibrantly colored vegetable dish uses a combination of turmeric and za'atar seasoning. Za'atar is a spice blend made from sesame seeds and herbs. Additionally, a touch of lemon acts to uplift the subduing qualities of turmeric. This one is ready in 30 minutes, and we use my quick tahini sauce to round out the flavors. I love to serve this with my Lamb Curry Meatballs (page 32).

Prep Time: 5 minutes
Cook Time: 25 minutes
Total Time: 30 minutes
Serves: 6

Preheat the oven to 425°F (220°C).

Make the cauliflower: In a large resealable plastic bag or large bowl, combine the cauliflower, olive oil, salt, pepper, turmeric, 2 teaspoons (5 g) of the za'atar and the coconut aminos. Shake or toss until all the cauliflower is covered with the mixture.

Place the cauliflower in the oven on the bottom rack for 25 minutes, tossing at about the 13-minute point.

Meanwhile, make the sauce: In a small bowl, combine the tahini, water, coconut aminos, lemon juice, cumin and salt, and whisk vigorously until smooth. Add more water for a thinner consistency.

Remove the cauliflower from the oven. Sprinkle the last teaspoon of za'atar over the cauliflower and toss. Drizzle with the sauce or serve it on the side. Garnish the cauliflower with parsley and red pepper flakes (if using).

Cauliflower

1 medium-sized head cauliflower, cut into bite-sized florets

3 tbsp (45 ml) olive oil

½ tsp salt

¼ tsp freshly ground black pepper

¼ tsp ground turmeric

1 tbsp (8 g) za'atar, divided

1 tbsp (15 ml) coconut aminos

Sauce

2 tbsp (30 g) unroasted or lightly roasted tahini

1 tbsp (15 ml) water

2 tsp (10 ml) coconut aminos

½ tsp fresh lemon juice

¼ tsp ground cumin

⅛ tsp salt

Optional Garnish

Chopped fresh parsley

Red pepper flakes

Simply Roasted Garlic-Paprika Broccolini

Paleo / Whole 30 / Egg Free / Gluten Free /
Dairy-Free Option / Nut Free / Vegan

Broccolini is similar to broccoli in nature, but with some clear differences. The stalks are thinner, the florets less dense and the flavor is not as domineering—perfect for adding flavorings to spruce up this simple yet desirable vegetable. Because the stalks are thinner, they cook quickly and this recipe cooks in only 15 minutes. My favorite way to prepare them is to pair them with salmon, steak or chicken. They also make for a great omelet or vegetable frittata.

Prep Time: 5 minutes
Cook Time: 15 minutes
Total Time: 20 minutes
Serves: 3 or 4

Preheat the oven to 425°F (220°C). Line a rimmed sheet pan with parchment paper.

Trim away ¼ inch (6 mm) from the ends of the broccolini, and place the broccolini in a large bowl. Add the smashed garlic and butter and toss to combine. Transfer to the prepared sheet pan. Sprinkle the broccolini with the salt, pepper and paprika and toss again.

Bake for 10 to 15 minutes, or until the broccolini is bright green and starts to char.

Remove from the oven and serve.

1 bunch broccolini

3 cloves garlic, smashed

2 tbsp (28 g) unsalted butter, ghee, or coconut oil, melted (use oil for dairy-free)

¼ tsp salt

Pinch of freshly ground black pepper

¼ tsp paprika

Lemon-Almond Asparagus

Paleo / Whole 30 / Egg Free / Gluten Free / Dairy Free / Vegan

I believe asparagus is at its best in springtime, when it is in season. It has a crisp, sweet note that, when combined with fresh lemon and crushed almonds, is quite refreshing and cleansing on the palate. This recipe is very simple yet full of flavor. Ready in under 15 minutes, it pairs well with a simple savory protein or fresh pasta salad.

Prep Time: 5 minutes
Cook Time: 10 minutes
Total Time: 15 minutes
Serves: 4

Preheat the oven to 400°F (200°C). Line a sheet pan with parchment paper.

On the prepared pan, combine the asparagus, olive oil, lemon slices, lemon juice, coconut aminos, salt, pepper and garlic. Toss evenly to coat, then spread evenly in a single layer.

Roast in the oven for 8 to 10 minutes, or until the asparagus is crisp on the outside and tender in the middle. Remove from the oven and top with the almonds.

1 lb (455 g) fresh asparagus, trimmed

1½ tbsp (22 ml) olive oil

½ lemon, thinly sliced

1 tbsp (15 ml) fresh lemon juice

1 tbsp (15 ml) coconut aminos

½ tsp sea salt

¼ tsp freshly ground black pepper

2 cloves garlic, sliced thinly

2 tbsp (14 g) chopped roasted almonds

Kale Apple Fennel Salad with Tahini-Dill Dressing

Paleo / Whole 30 / Egg Free / Gluten Free / Dairy Free / Vegan

Kale is one of my go-to greens. The key to using it raw is to massage it to break down the fiber, making it tender. For this salad, I use olive oil to do so. I also use a mandoline to slice the apple, fennel and onion, to create a sense of uniformity. A fennel bulb may look like onion when chopped, but it is far more sweet than pungent. It contains a mild property that stimulates digestion, preparing your body for the next course. Quick and simple, this salad and dressing are ready in just 15 minutes.

Prep Time: 15 minutes
Cook Time: 0 minutes
Total Time: 15 minutes
Serves: 4 to 6

Make the dressing: In a high-speed blender, combine all the dressing ingredients: water, tahini, lemon juice, coconut aminos, dill, olive oil, balsamic vinegar, garlic, salt and pepper. Blend until very smooth. Add more water if you want it thinner. Set aside.

Make the salad: Place the kale in a large bowl, add the olive oil and, using your hands, massage the oil into the kale for about 30 seconds, or until the kale has softened and is coated with the oil. Set aside.

Using a mandoline or a sharp knife, thinly slice the apple, then slice the slices into thirds.

With the same mandoline or knife, slice the red onion and fennel bulb. Be careful of your fingers when using a mandoline, as you could easily cut yourself.

Add the apple, red onion, fennel, figs and walnuts to the kale, and toss using your hands or a salad tosser. Add the salt and toss again.

Toss the salad with your preferred amount of dressing, or serve the dressing on the side. Garnish with hemp seeds and red pepper flakes (if using).

You can store the undressed salad in the fridge for 1 to 2 days. The dressing will keep separately in the fridge for 7 to 10 days.

Dressing

¼ cup (60 ml) water

7 tbsp (105 g) unroasted or lightly roasted tahini

3 tbsp (45 ml) fresh lemon juice

2 tbsp (30 ml) coconut aminos

2 tbsp (8 g) chopped fresh dill

1 tbsp (15 ml) olive oil

1 tbsp (15 ml) balsamic vinegar

1 medium-sized clove garlic, chopped

¼ tsp salt

⅛ tsp freshly ground black pepper

Salad

1 large head lacinato or regular kale, rinsed, dried and chopped

1 tbsp (15 ml) olive oil

½ large Fuji or Honeycrisp apple, washed (about ½ cup [55 g] once mandolined)

¼ medium-sized red onion (⅓ cup [40 g] once mandolined)

½ small fennel bulb, rinsed (¼ cup [22 g] once mandolined)

¼ cup (38 g) halved dried figs

2 tbsp (15 g) chopped walnuts

¼ tsp salt

Hemp seeds (optional)

Red pepper flakes (optional)

Marinated Lettuce-Free Greek Salad

This lettuce-free salad is perfect for meal prep, because the ingredients are able to marinate and fuse their flavors together each day in the fridge. The secret to success with this salad is all about the chopping technique and ensuring each component is similar in size, allowing you to capture a little of everything with every bite. I prefer goat milk feta, but any feta, including dairy-free, will work. The dressing is a simple blended vinaigrette. It is perfect for a summer picnic or outdoor barbecue, or as a quick lunch or dinner when adding a protein of choice. This salad requires no oven and takes just 15 minutes to prepare.

Prep Time: 15 minutes
Cook Time: 0 minutes
Total Time: 15 minutes
Serves: 8

Make the salad: In a large bowl, combine the cucumber, tomatoes, bell pepper, red onion, feta cheese, olives and parsley. Toss, then set aside.

Make the dressing: In a high-speed blender, combine the water, olive oil, lemon juice, coconut aminos, vinegar, garlic, oregano, mustard, dill, salt, black pepper and red pepper flakes. Blend for about 30 seconds, or until smooth.

Pour your preferred amount of dressing over the salad and toss again.

Place any extra dressing in the fridge; it will keep for 7 to 10 days refrigerated.

Salad

1 English cucumber, seeded and cut into quarter-moons

1 pint (300 g) cherry tomatoes, halved

1 bell pepper, seeded and chopped

½ medium-sized red onion, diced

8 oz (225 g) feta cheese, cut into cubes (use dairy-free for vegan)

1 cup (180 g) pitted Kalamata olives, halved

2 tbsp (8 g) chopped fresh parsley

Dressing

¼ cup (60 ml) water

6 tbsp (90 ml) olive oil

2 tbsp (30 ml) fresh lemon juice

1 tbsp (15 ml) coconut aminos

1 tbsp (15 ml) apple cider vinegar

1 clove garlic, chopped

½ tsp dried oregano

½ tsp Dijon mustard

½ tsp chopped fresh dill

½ tsp kosher salt

¼ tsp freshly ground black pepper

Pinch of red pepper flakes

Watermelon Avocado Cucumber Salad

Paleo / Whole 30 Option / Egg Free / Gluten Free
Dairy Free / Nut Free / Vegan Option

This recipe screams "summer." It is aesthetically pleasing, light and refreshing with hints of lime, mint and cilantro. It is another one of those sides that gets even more flavorful as it marinates. I love using the juice that is left over when the salad is gone to marinate chicken or pour over some greens. This dish is perfect for a summer barbecue, coming together in 15 minutes with no cooking required.

Prep Time: 15 minutes
Cook Time: 0 minutes
Total Time: 15 minutes
Serves: 8

In a small bowl, mix together the salt, pepper and paprika. Set aside.

In a separate small bowl, mix together the lime juice, coconut aminos and honey. Set aside.

In a large bowl, combine the watermelon, avocados, cucumber, scallion, cilantro and mint, and toss. Next, add the spice mixture to the salad and toss again, making sure to evenly coat the ingredients. Finally, add the lime mixture to the salad and toss again.

Keep refrigerated until ready to serve. The dressed salad will keep for 1 to 2 days in the refrigerator.

½ tsp salt

¼ tsp freshly ground black pepper

½ tsp paprika

1 tbsp (15 ml) fresh lime juice

1 tbsp (15 ml) coconut aminos

1 tsp honey (sub pure maple syrup for vegan or omit for Whole 30)

5 cups (750 g) chopped watermelon (chopped into small, uniform cubes)

2 medium-sized avocados, peeled, pitted and chopped into cubes

1 English cucumber, quartered and then chopped

1 large scallion, chopped

2 tbsp (5 g) minced fresh cilantro

1 tbsp (3 g) minced fresh mint

DELIGHTFUL PROTEIN-PACKED
Apps

"You know, if there's no room, then I guess you and I will have to just finish the plate," said my grandfather as he was scanning the platter of gigantic shrimp cocktail I was holding while searching for a space to put my dish down among the many other platters, finger foods, dips and Christmas cookies. I couldn't even see the festive tablecloth covering our 12-foot (3.7-m)-long cherrywood dining room table. When it comes to hosting parties, my family goes all out on the food. This special night was our annual Christmas Eve party, and it was a big deal. My relatives would fly in for the holiday, and more than 50 people would fill the house the night before Christmas. There were never any traditional meals, just endless amounts of appetizers, finger foods and a wide selection of cookies and desserts.

To this day, I have a special place in my heart for cocktail-style parties. For one thing, I love the idea of everyone getting to try a bite of everything. No one is confined to just one dish. I've talked previously about the power that food holds—I think its most significant power is how it brings people together, in a joyful manner. It never fails to stimulate conversation! As a kid, I always helped with kitchen prep before a big private party. My first job: the designated shrimp peeler. I could peel and devein a shrimp like a professional by the age of ten.

As I grew older, I became a cohost, and by my high school years, half of that 12-foot (3.7-m)-long table was filled with my very own culinary contributions. As everyone filled their plates to the brim, the conversations about the food took over, guests raving about their favorites as they reached for more. "Don't let me leave without getting the recipe!" I would hear. As the years went on, more often than not, they were talking to me.

For this chapter, I have rounded up a variety of my most requested appetizer recipes from over the years— packed with both nutrients and flavor. As much as I love to host, I try to keep it simple. In case you are a seafood lover like me, I've shared two versions of shrimp cocktail: my classic (page 95), along with my Mexican-inspired version (page 96). I also included my shrimp appetizer balls with their seriously addictive and healthy sesame ginger dipping sauce (page 92). You will also find my heart-healthy deviled eggs (page 88), made with creamy ripe avocado. I guarantee, this chapter has something you will love, whether you are hosting a party, contributing to a menu or feel like a tapas-style dinner!

Smoked Salmon Platter with White Bean Dip

Egg Free / Gluten Free / Dairy Free / Nut Free

Smoked salmon has always been a part of our family functions. While I was growing up, we always served it with fresh lemon, dill, capers and rye bread. Over the years, I created my own twist and made it into a customizable appetizer. I prefer to lighten it up with cucumber slices and create more of a charcuterie-style platter, which is enjoyable and interactive for everyone. No cooking required here and it's ready in 15 minutes.

Prep Time: 15 minutes
Cook Time: 0 minutes
Total Time: 15 minutes
Makes: 6 to 8 appetizer servings

Make the dip: In a high-speed blender or food processor, combine the white beans, olive oil, lemon juice, garlic, salt, black pepper and lemon zest, and blend until smooth.

Pour the dip into a bowl and mix in the dill. Place a small amount of the dip in a smaller bowl or ramekin.

Assemble the platter: Place the capers and olives in their own separate smaller oyster cups. On a board, large plate or sheet pan lined with parchment paper, arrange the salmon, cucumber, red onion, tomato and lemon slices. I like to separate these so each ingredient has its own section.

Garnish the platter with fresh dill and red pepper flakes. Drizzle olive oil over the dip. Add extra crackers and/or bread and other veggies (if using) and more capers on the side. Serve with some small utensils to allow your guests to top the salmon with the red onion and capers. The salmon can be served on its own or on top of the cucumber or crackers and/or bread. Use the crackers and/or bread and veggies for the dip and serve olives as a little extra snack. Refill the ramekin with the extra dip as necessary.

White Bean Dip

1 (16-oz [455-g]) can white beans, drained and rinsed

¼ cup (60 ml) olive oil, plus more for drizzling

2 tbsp (30 ml) fresh lemon juice

1 clove garlic, chopped

½ tsp salt

¼ tsp freshly ground black pepper

¼ tsp lemon zest

1 tbsp (4 g) chopped fresh dill

Platter

2 to 3 tbsp (17 to 26 g) capers, plus more for garnish

¼ cup (45 g) olives

8 oz (225 g) cold smoked wild salmon

1 English cucumber, sliced thinly

½ medium-sized red onion, sliced thinly

1 medium-sized tomato, sliced

1 lemon, sliced thinly

Fresh dill, for garnish

Red pepper flakes, for garnish

Crackers and/or bread of choice (optional; gluten-free, if necessary)

Other veggies, such as carrots or peppers (optional)

Avocado Deviled Eggs

Paleo / Whole 30 / Gluten Free / Dairy Free / Nut Free

This Mexican twist on a classic American appetizer is always a hit for a crowd. The avocado creates a velvety texture, adds fiber and is packed with nutrients. It tastes delicious with the addition of a couple of surprising ingredients, including cumin and grated onion. There is something addictive about these flavors that keeps a crowd coming back for seconds. I like to top each egg with a touch of crispy bacon and a slice of fresh jalapeño.

> Prep Time: 15 minutes
> Cook Time: 12 minutes
> Total Time: 27 minutes
> Makes: 20 deviled egg halves

Fill a medium-sized saucepan with the eggs and enough water to cover. Bring to a boil, cover and turn off the heat. Let the eggs sit for 12 minutes.

Meanwhile, in a small bowl, mix together the avocado, onion, mayo, lemon and lime juices, coconut aminos, chopped jalapeño, cumin, lemon zest and salt and black pepper to taste.

Fill a large bowl with cold water and add ice. When the eggs are done, immediately transfer them to the bowl and leave them there for 3 minutes, for an ice water bath.

Once the eggs are cooled, crack and remove the shells, then slice each egg in half. Scoop out the yolks, mash and mix them into the avocado mixture.

Fill a resealable plastic bag with the mixture and cut a small hole in a corner, or use a pastry bag. Fill the egg whites equally with the mixture. Top with slices of cooked bacon, the cilantro, jalapeños and red pepper flakes (if using).

10 large eggs

1 ripe avocado, peeled, pitted and mashed

1 tbsp (10 g) grated onion

1 tbsp (14 g) mayonnaise (use Paleo-friendly for Paleo- or Whole 30–friendly)

1 tbsp (15 ml) fresh lemon juice

1 tbsp (15 ml) fresh lime juice

1 tsp coconut aminos

1 to 2 tsp (3 to 6 g) finely chopped jalapeño pepper

½ tsp ground cumin

½ tsp lemon zest

Salt and freshly ground black pepper

2 slices cooked bacon, cut into ½-inch (1.3-cm) pieces, for topping

Fresh cilantro, for topping (optional)

Sliced jalapeño peppers, for topping (optional)

Red pepper flakes, for topping (optional)

Asian Turkey Meatballs

Paleo Option / Gluten Free / Dairy Free / Nut Free

I'm a big fan of Asian flavors and love the marriage of ginger and scallions. These turkey-based meatballs are packed with robust Asian flavors and served with a lightly sweet and salty ginger scallion tamari dipping sauce. They are gluten free, as I have replaced the bread crumbs with mushrooms, which stabilize the moisture and add to the retention of flavor. Like all my meatballs, these are prepped in under 10 minutes and spend the rest of the time in the oven.

Prep Time: 10 minutes
Cook Time: 20 minutes
Total Time: 30 minutes
Makes: About 14 meatballs

Preheat the oven to 400°F (200°C). Line a sheet pan with parchment paper.

Make the meatballs: In a large bowl, combine the turkey, egg, mushrooms, cilantro, scallions, tamari, ginger, sesame oil, salt and black pepper. Using clean hands, mix together until well mixed.

Form into 1½-inch (4-cm)-diameter balls and place the meatballs about 1½ inches (4 cm) apart on the prepared sheet pan (you may need two pans). Bake the meatballs for 20 minutes.

Meanwhile, make the sauce: In a small saucepan, combine the coconut sugar and water and bring to a boil. Add the coconut aminos, tamari, lime juice, ginger, garlic and red pepper flakes, and lower the heat to medium. Let the sauce simmer for 12 to 15 minutes, or until slightly reduced. Remove the sauce from the heat and pour into a bowl.

When the meatballs are done, remove from the oven and transfer them to a plate. Serve with the sauce, garnishing with more chopped scallions, cilantro and sesame seeds, if you'd like.

Meatballs

1 lb (455 g) ground turkey (93% lean)

1 large egg, lightly beaten

¾ cup (53 g) minced mushrooms

½ cup (20 g) finely chopped fresh cilantro

¼ cup (24 g) chopped scallions

1 tbsp (15 ml) tamari (sub coconut aminos for Paleo)

1 tsp grated fresh ginger

1 tsp sesame oil

¼ tsp salt

¼ tsp freshly ground black pepper

Sauce

¼ cup (55 g) coconut sugar or raw cane sugar

3 tbsp (45 ml) water

¼ cup (60 ml) coconut aminos

¼ cup (60 ml) tamari (sub coconut aminos for Paleo)

¼ cup (60 ml) fresh lime juice

2 tbsp (12 g) minced fresh ginger

3 cloves garlic, minced

Pinch of red pepper flakes

Optional Garnish

Chopped scallions

Chopped cilantro

Sesame seeds

Shrimp Dumpling Balls with Cashew Dipping Sauce

Paleo Option / Whole 30 Option / Egg Free / Gluten Free / Dairy Free

As a shellfish lover, I am always searching for fresh ideas. The inspiration for this appetizer came from one of my favorite classics: a shrimp dumpling. My twist is not only gluten free but grain free as well. These bite-sized balls are made with no fillers. The result is a tender, flavorful, guilt-free appetizer bite with a dipping sauce that is to die for. Plus, they are ready in 25 minutes.

Prep Time: 10 minutes
Cook Time: 15 minutes
Total Time: 25 minutes
Makes: 10 balls

Preheat the oven to 350°F (180°C). Line a sheet pan with parchment paper.

Make the shrimp dumplings: Place the shrimp in a food processor and process for about 30 seconds (the result will be a sticky paste). Scrape into a medium-sized bowl.

Add the ginger, salt, olive oil, cilantro, onion and tamari, then whisk in the egg white. Using a fork, mix the ingredients together to ensure they are well combined.

Spoon 1½ tablespoons (50 g) per ball onto the prepared pan and shape them into balls. Bake for 15 minutes, or until they are firm.

Meanwhile, make the sauce: In a small bowl, combine the coconut milk, cashew butter, date syrup, sriracha, coconut aminos, lime juice, tamari, salt, ginger and sesame oil (if using). Whisk together until smooth.

Remove the shrimp balls from the oven and serve with the sauce. Garnish with the sesame seeds and chopped scallions, and serve with fresh cilantro and lime wedges, if you wish.

1 lb (455 g) shrimp, peeled and deveined

½ tsp minced fresh ginger

¼ tsp salt

1 tsp olive oil

1 tbsp (3 g) chopped cilantro

½ onion, minced

1 tsp tamari (sub coconut aminos for Paleo or Whole 30)

1 large egg white

Sauce

3 tbsp (45 ml) coconut milk

2 tbsp (32 g) cashew butter

2 tbsp (40 g) date syrup or honey (use date syrup for Whole 30)

1 tbsp (15 ml) sriracha

1 tbsp (15 ml) coconut aminos

1½ tsp (scant 8 ml) fresh lime juice

½ tsp tamari (sub Paleo-friendly Asian fish sauce, such as Red Boat brand, for Paleo or Whole 30)

⅛ tsp salt

⅛ tsp ground ginger

Drop of sesame oil (optional)

Sesame seeds, chopped scallions, fresh cilantro and lime wedges, for serving (optional)

Shrimp Cocktail Two Ways

Paleo Option / Whole 30 Option / Egg Free / Gluten Free
Dairy Free / Nut Free

When I arrive at a function, I scan the table for my all-time favorite appetizer: jumbo-sized shrimp cocktail. When making my own, I like to add a hint of flavor to the shrimp by cooking them in a quick broth. This small extra step really elevates the taste. Here, I share two versions: Classic Shrimp Cocktail with a Paleo-friendly homemade dip, and my Mexican Shrimp Cocktail served over a sauce made from salsa, avocado and mangoes. These babies cook in just 3 minutes and the entire appetizer is ready to serve in 30.

Prep Time: 8 minutes
Cook Time: 22 minutes
Total Time: 30 minutes
Makes: 4 to 6 appetizer servings

Classic Shrimp Cocktail

Make the shrimp: In a large saucepan, combine the water, coconut sugar and salt. Squeeze the lemon juice into the pan and add the squeezed lemon halves. Bring to a boil, stir to dissolve the sugar and salt, then turn off the heat.

Add the shrimp and allow to cook in the water for 3½ minutes. Immediately add the ice to stop the shrimp from cooking further. Allow to sit in the ice water for 10 minutes.

While the shrimp cools, make the cocktail sauce: In a medium-sized bowl, combine the ketchup, lemon juice, coconut aminos, horseradish, date syrup, sriracha, salt and pepper and whisk together.

Remove the shrimp from the ice water; pat dry. Serve with the sauce, extra lemons and parsley.

Shrimp

6 cups (1.4 L) water

2 tbsp (28 g) coconut sugar (use 4 chopped dates for Whole 30)

2 tbsp (32 g) salt

1 lemon, halved

1 lb (455 g) wild jumbo shrimp, peeled and deveined

8 cups (1.1 kg) ice

Cocktail Sauce

½ cup (120 g) organic ketchup (for Paleo or Whole 30, use date-sweetened or unsweetened ketchup)

1 tbsp (15 ml) fresh lemon juice

1 tbsp (15 ml) coconut aminos

1 tbsp (15 g) prepared horseradish

1 tbsp (20 g) date syrup or honey (use date syrup for Whole 30)

½ to 1 tsp sriracha (depending on how spicy you want it)

¼ tsp salt

Pinch of freshly ground black pepper

For Serving

Additional lemons

Chopped fresh parsley

Mexican Shrimp Cocktail

Peel the mango and reserve the peel for cooking the shrimp; set the rest of the mango aside for the salsa.

Make the shrimp: In a large saucepan, combine the water, coconut sugar and salt. Squeeze the lime juice into the pan and add the squeezed lime halves along with the reserved mango skin. Bring to a boil, stir to dissolve the sugar and salt, then turn off the heat.

Add the shrimp and allow to cook in the water for 3½ minutes. Immediately add the ice to stop the shrimp from cooking further. Allow the shrimp to sit in ice water for 10 minutes.

While the shrimp cools, make the salsa: Pit and chop the reserved mango. In a medium-sized bowl, combine the mango, avocado, tomato, onion, cilantro, jalapeño pepper, salt and black pepper, and mix well to combine.

Add the lime juice and mix again.

Remove the shrimp from the ice water; pat dry.

Top with scallions and cilantro and serve with tortilla chips and extra limes. To enjoy, scoop a little salsa on top of the shrimp and use tortilla chips to scoop extra salsa.

Prep Time: 8 minutes
Cook Time: 22 minutes
Total Time: 30 minutes
Makes: 6 to 8 appetizer servings

1 ripe mango

Shrimp

6 cups (1.4 L) water

2 tbsp (28 g) coconut sugar (use 4 chopped dates for Whole 30)

2 tbsp (36 g) salt

1 lime, halved

1 lb (455 g) jumbo wild shrimp, peeled and deveined

8 cups (1.1 kg) ice

Avocado Mango Salsa

1 avocado, peeled, pitted and chopped into chunks

1 medium-sized ripe tomato, chopped

½ medium-sized red onion, diced

3 tbsp (8 g) chopped fresh cilantro

1 tbsp (9 g) minced jalapeño pepper

½ tsp salt

¼ tsp freshly ground black pepper

Juice of 1 lime

For Serving

Scallions, for topping

Fresh cilantro, for topping

Tortilla chips

Additional limes

Blueberry Oat Buckwheat Pancakes

I have a lot of pancake recipes, but this one has a special place in my heart. It's the first gluten-free pancake recipe I ever created. I use buckwheat flour and quick-cooking gluten-free oats in this recipe. It is a hearty take on a classic blueberry pancake that takes only 10 minutes from start to finish. My favorite way to serve this one is topped with some grass-fed butter and maple syrup.

Prep Time: 5 minutes
Cook Time: 5 minutes
Total Time: 10 minutes
Serves: 6 to 8

In a high-speed blender, blend 1½ cups (120 g) of the oats into a flour, about 45 seconds. In a medium-sized bowl, mix together the blended oats, remaining cup (80 g) of oats, buckwheat flour, coconut flour, baking soda, baking powder, cinnamon and salt.

Make a well in the center, and add the eggs, coconut oil, coconut milk, maple syrup and vanilla, then whisk until incorporated and smooth. Using a large spoon, fold in the blueberries.

Heat a lightly oiled griddle or skillet over medium-high heat.

Pour or scoop ¼ cup (60 ml) of batter for each pancake. Once the tops begin to bubble, flip the pancakes.

Cook for another minute, or until cooked through (if you gently press the center, the pancake should spring back). Serve with the butter and maple syrup if you'd like.

2½ cups (200 g) old-fashioned oats, divided (gluten-free, if needed)

½ cup (60 g) buckwheat flour

2 tbsp (14 g) coconut flour

1 tsp baking soda

1 tsp baking powder

½ tsp ground cinnamon

Pinch of salt

2 large eggs

1 tbsp (14 g) coconut oil, melted, plus more for griddle

1 cup (240 ml) coconut milk

2 tbsp (30 ml) pure maple syrup

1½ tsp (scant 8 ml) vanilla extract

1 cup (155 g) frozen wild blueberries

Oil, for griddle

Optional Toppings

Butter (omit for dairy-free)

Maple syrup

Easy Salsa Shakshuka

Paleo / Whole 30 Option / Gluten Free / Dairy Free / Nut Free / Keto

Shakshuka has been a classic Mediterranean dish for centuries. My take on this savory breakfast is replacing the traditional spicy tomato sauce with your salsa of preference. I personally prefer a chunky salsa over a smooth texture. The salsa simplifies the traditional recipe and gives it a fun Mexican flair, especially paired with fresh avocado and tortilla chips for scooping. Plus, you can enjoy this in less than 15 minutes.

Prep Time: 2 minutes
Cook Time: 12 minutes
Total Time: 14 minutes
Serves: 1 or 2

In an 8-inch (20.5-cm) skillet with a lid (I prefer cast iron), heat the salsa over medium-high heat for about 3 minutes, or until the salsa is bubbling.

Crack the eggs into the salsa, spacing them apart equally. Cook the eggs for 3 to 4 minutes, spooning off any additional liquid that may rise. You should be able to see the whites about half cooked at this point.

Lower the heat to medium and cover the pan. Cook for 4 to 5 minutes longer, or until the whites are cooked through. If you want more of a sunny-side up egg, remove the lid to allow steam out every 20 seconds or so. This extra step keeps the tops of the eggs from overcooking.

Remove from the heat. Top with your choice of toppings.

1½ cups (390 g) salsa

3 large eggs

Optional Toppings

Fresh tomatoes

Sliced avocado

Fresh cilantro

Chopped scallions

Tortilla chips (Paleo if needed, omit for Whole 30)

Sweet Potato "Toast"

Paleo / Whole 30 / Egg Free / Gluten Free / Dairy Free / Nut Free / Vegan

Sweet potatoes pair well with both sweet and savory toppings. If you follow me on Instagram ((@starinfinitefood), you will know that sweet potato toast is one of my favorite ways to celebrate #toasttuesday. This is a fun recipe that is Paleo- and Whole 30–friendly and can be adapted to vegan and vegetarian lifestyles. It replaces traditional toast with a more nutrient-dense starch. This toast alternative takes only 3 minutes to prep and is ready in under 30. They freeze well and can be popped into a toaster or oven when you're ready to enjoy them for added convenience.

Prep Time: 5 minutes
Cook Time: 24 minutes
Total Time: 29 minutes
Serves: 4

Preheat the oven to 425°F (220°C).

Slice the sweet potatoes lengthwise to about ⅓ inch (8.3 mm) thick. To do so, hold the potato steady with your hand, and using a sharp knife, make the markings to measure the desired thickness. Carefully slice straight down until the entire potato is sliced, then brush both sides with olive oil.

Place the sweet potatoes in the oven on the bottom rack, directly onto the rack, skin side down. Sprinkle the tops of the sweet potatoes with the salt, and bake for 22 to 24 minutes, flipping at about the 11-minute point. They should be slightly browned on each side and tender in the middle.

Top with your favorite toast toppings and serve.

1 lb (455 g) sweet potatoes
2 tsp (10 ml) olive oil
⅛ tsp salt

Sweet Topping Ideas
Yogurt (dairy-free if needed)
Fresh fruit
Nut butter (omit for nut free)
Granola (gluten-, nut-, dairy-free and/or Paleo if needed)
Jam

Savory Topping Ideas
Prosciutto (omit for vegan)
Fresh greens
Smoked salmon (omit for vegan)
Avocado
Hummus (omit for Paleo/Whole 30)
Fried eggs (omit for vegan)
Beans (omit for Paleo/Whole 30)
Roasted veggies
Pesto (dairy-free and/or nut-free if needed)

Four-Ingredient Plantain Pancake Pizza

Great for weekend brunch, this giant pancake divides like a pizza, making it quite an enjoyable experience for everyone at the table. It's prepared on the stovetop and finished in the oven. No flipping is required and it's ready in 10 minutes. Just as with pizza, you can create your own masterpiece, such as half sweet, half savory. Did I mention you can eat it with your hands? Ripe plantains offer a similar texture to bananas, but with a more neutral flavor, making them a perfect ingredient to use in baked goods.

Prep Time: 5 minutes
Cook Time: 5 minutes
Total Time: 10 minutes
Serves: 2

Set the oven broiler to high.

In a high-speed blender, combine the plantain, eggs, coconut flour and baking soda, and blend until smooth. It should be a thick batter, but still spreadable.

Heat a 9-inch (23-cm) cast-iron or oven-safe pan over medium heat. Oil the pan with the coconut oil, making sure to oil it well so the pancake won't stick.

Once the pan is hot, pour in the batter and spread it with a rubber spatula or the back of a large spoon to cover the entire pan.

Cook the pancake over medium heat for 2 to 3 minutes, or until you see bubbles on the top. Then, place the pan on a rack 6 inches (15 cm) under the broiler. Broil for about 2 minutes, or until the top begins to brown and the pancake feels stiff and cooked through.

Remove the pan from the broiler and flip the pancake onto a plate. Top with your desired toppings.

1 large ripe plantain
2 large eggs
2 tbsp (14 g) coconut flour
½ tsp baking soda
Coconut oil, for pan

Topping Ideas

Plain yogurt (dairy-free, if needed)
Nut butter (omit for nut-free, or use seed butter)
Fresh fruit
Granola (gluten-, dairy-free and/or Paleo if needed)
Pure maple syrup
Sliced avocado
Hemp seeds

Mini Gluten-Free Blueberry Muffins

Gluten Free / Dairy-Free Option

I choose to let lightly sweetened blueberries do the heavy lifting for these delicious bite-sized muffins. These are perfect for busy mornings on the go and take under 30 minutes to make. They are also travel- and freezer-friendly. For a well-rounded breakfast, I love to top off a bowl of yogurt with a couple of these mini muffins and some almond butter. If you love classic blueberry muffins, you are sure to love this whole-food twist.

Prep Time: 10 minutes
Cook Time: 18 minutes
Total Time: 28 minutes
Makes: 24 mini muffins or 16 regular-sized muffins

Preheat the oven to 350°F (180°C).

In a large bowl, combine the white rice flour, millet flour, almond flour, cassava flour, tapioca flour, baking powder, baking soda and salt. Whisk together until well mixed. Set aside.

In a stand mixer or a separate large bowl, combine the eggs, almond butter, coconut sugar, applesauce, vanilla and yogurt. Using the stand mixer or a whisk, mix well until smooth. Add the dry ingredients to the wet and whisk until well combined.

Using a wooden spoon or large metal spoon, fold in the blueberries.

Line a 24-well mini muffin tin with muffin liners or oil with coconut oil, then divide the batter equally among the wells. Bake for 16 to 18 minutes, until a toothpick inserted into the center of a muffin comes out clean.

Note: If you prefer regular-sized muffins, prepare 16 regular-sized muffin wells, fill as above and bake for an additional 5 to 7 minutes.

½ cup (79 g) white rice flour
½ cup (80 g) millet flour
½ cup (50 g) almond flour
2 tbsp (8 g) cassava flour
1 tbsp (8 g) tapioca flour
2 tsp (9 g) baking powder
½ tsp baking soda
½ tsp fine sea salt
2 large eggs
¼ cup (65 g) creamy almond butter
½ cup (113 g) coconut sugar
½ cup (125 g) applesauce
2 tsp (10 ml) vanilla extract
2 tbsp (30 g) Greek yogurt (dairy-free, if needed)
1 cup (145 g) fresh or frozen blueberries, plus a few more to top
Coconut oil, for pan (optional)

Vegan Carrot Raisin Muffins

Egg Free / Gluten-Free Option / Dairy Free / Vegan

These muffins are vegan, gluten-free and banana-free and have that same bakery-style flavor you'd expect from a morning glory muffin. I use a unique method of steaming the carrots instead of shredding them. These muffins also have notes of cinnamon and cardamom. I enjoy topping them with raspberry jam to start my morning on the right foot. They take only 30 minutes and are great to prep ahead for busy mornings.

Prep Time: 8 minutes
Cook Time: 22 minutes
Total Time: 30 minutes
Makes: 9 to 10 muffins

Preheat the oven to 375°F (190°C).

In a small cup, combine the chia seeds and ⅓ cup (80 ml) of water. Set aside for 5 minutes until the mixture thickens into a gel.

In a large bowl, whisk together the oats, flour, baking soda, baking powder, salt, cinnamon and cardamom.

In a medium-sized bowl, whisk together the almond butter, vanilla and maple syrup.

Place the carrots in a high-speed blender along with ½ cup (120 ml) of water. Blend until a puree forms.

Transferring the flour mixture to a stand mixer or leaving it in its large bowl, add the almond butter mixture, the soaked chia seeds and the carrot puree to the flour mixture and mix on medium-high speed with the stand mixer or a hand mixer until a batter is formed and all the ingredients are well mixed. Fold in the raisins by hand.

Oil 10 wells of a muffin pan with coconut oil or line with muffin liners. Depending on the size of your muffin pans, you may end up with 9 or 10 muffins. Pour in the batter, dividing it evenly among the prepared wells and filling each well almost to the top. Bake on the bottom rack for 20 to 22 minutes, or until a toothpick inserted into the center of a muffin comes out clean.

Note: You can substitute the canned carrots for 1 heaping cup (about 5.5 ounces [150 g]) of chopped fresh carrots. In a small saucepan, combine the carrots with 2 cups (475 ml) of water and bring to a boil. Cover and allow to cook for 5 to 7 minutes; the carrots should be pierced easily with a fork.

2 tbsp (20 g) chia seeds

1 cup (80 g) old-fashioned oats (gluten-free, if needed)

1 cup (124 g) 1:1 gluten-free flour blend (I use King Arthur brand Measure for Measure)

1 tsp baking soda

1 tsp baking powder

½ tsp salt

½ tsp ground cinnamon

¼ tsp ground cardamom

½ cup (130 g) creamy almond butter

1 tsp vanilla extract

⅓ cup (80 ml) pure maple syrup

1 (8.25-oz [234-g]) can no-salt-added sliced carrots, drained (about 1 heaping cup [150 g])

½ cup (75 g) raisins

Coconut oil, for pan (optional)

NUTRITIOUS, STARCHY
Sides

"Tiny dices, and they all need to be uniform." My brother Mike's words were repeating in my head. I had spent the day holding the largest kitchen knife I had ever held in my life, dicing potatoes with ice-cold hands. It was January in New England, and the building where my brother and dad had started their clam chowder venture was not heated. I was 24 years old and had just left my job a few months earlier when my dad got sick. He passed away six weeks later, just a couple of months after he and my brother decided to go into business to market Mike's award-winning chowder on a wholesale level. After my dad passed, my brother John and I stepped in to help keep the business going. For the next few months, I would lose myself in this culinary task about four days a week.

One of those nights after a day spent chopping, I quickly scanned the kitchen only to find there was very little food in the house. I decided to chop up a bunch of large potatoes, boil them, smash them and bake them in oil and a bunch of seasonings. At the time, I was living with my boyfriend and his two children who were two of the pickiest eaters I had ever cooked for. It was always a gamble making dinner, never knowing how they were going to react to their plates. But I liked the challenge.

Anytime I have found myself in a dark place throughout my life, cooking has always been my therapy. This time was no different. That night the kids ended up going crazy for those crispy little potato bites, calling them "Catie's Tots" as they smothered them in ketchup. When you find a good kid-friendly recipe, you hold on to it! Plus, I loved it, too.

In this chapter, I have rounded out a selection of my favorite starchy sides, one of the best parts of a meal, if you ask me. I mean, who doesn't love carbs?! I've taken many of my favorites and created simple, quicker versions that can be made in under 30 minutes.

I refined my recipe for "Catie's Tots" over the years and made them even better using baby new potatoes. You'll find "Catie's Tots" now listed as "Crispy Garlic Smashed Potatoes" (page 123). You'll also find a few of my other favorite potato recipes and my Lighter Mango-Coconut Rice (page 131), which was inspired by a dish I used to order when I visited my dad when he lived in Costa Rica. Whether you're cooking for the holidays or preparing weeknight family dinner, I promise there's the perfect hearty and healthy starch to round off that plate.

Crispy Garlic Smashed Potatoes

Paleo Option / Whole 30 Option / Egg Free / Gluten Free
Dairy-Free Option / Nut Free / Vegan Option

This one is a kid favorite. It has that ideal crispy exterior and soft interior. A perfect finger food that is a cross between french fries and baked potato. No cutting involved; just boil the potatoes with a splash of olive oil and seasoning, then smash and bake them for 20 minutes. I personally love to dip them in some ketchup, sour cream or my avocado pesto, to add some extra flavor punch (see Avocado Pesto Potato Salad, page 136).

Prep Time: 8 minutes
Cook Time: 20 minutes
Total Time: 28 minutes
Serves: 4

Place the potatoes in a medium-sized saucepan and cover with water by about an inch (2.5 cm). Add the salt. Bring to a boil, cover and cook for 8 minutes, or until you can pierce a potato with a fork.

Meanwhile, in a small sauté pan, heat the olive oil and garlic until very hot (it should begin to splatter). Lower the heat and cook for 1 minute, then turn off the heat.

In a small bowl, mix together the thyme and onion powder. Set aside.

When the potatoes are done, drain and place them on a cutting board or flat surface. Pat dry with a paper towel. With the bottom of a flat cup, gently press down and smash them.

Set the oven broiler to low. Line a sheet pan with a piece of aluminum foil or a silicone sheet (do not use parchment paper).

Transfer the potatoes to the prepared sheet pan. Discard the garlic from the oil, then drizzle the oil over the potatoes and season with half the seasoning mix. Turn each potato over, making sure that it is covered with oil, then season them with the rest of the seasoning mix. Sprinkle with a little pepper to taste.

Place the sheet pan 6 inches (15 cm) from the broiler. Broil for about 4 minutes, or until the tops begin to crisp. Flip each potato and broil for 4 more minutes.

Top the potatoes with the cheese, some chopped fresh parsley and scallions if you'd like. Serve with your choice of dipping sauce.

1 lb (455 g) baby new potatoes
½ tsp salt
3 tbsp (45 ml) olive oil
3 cloves garlic, chopped
½ tsp dried thyme
½ tsp onion powder
Freshly ground black pepper

Optional Toppings
Parmesan cheese (omit for Paleo, Whole 30, dairy-free or vegan)
Chopped fresh parsley
Chopped scallions

Honey Mustard Dill Potatoes

Paleo / Egg Free / Gluten Free / Dairy-Free Option / Nut Free

Honey mustard is one of those nostalgic flavors that brings me back to summer day barbecues. For this recipe, you'll coat the potatoes with the sauce before roasting or frying. The result leaves a caramelized exterior from the honey and coconut aminos. These potatoes pair well with just about any protein in your refrigerator, and they take only 30 minutes from start to finish.

Prep Time: 5 minutes
Cook Time: 25 minutes
Total Time: 30 minutes
Serves: 4

Preheat the oven to 425°F (220°C). Line a sheet pan with parchment paper.

In a medium-sized bowl, combine the mustard, butter, dill, salt, pepper, honey, garlic and coconut aminos. Mix well.

Add the potatoes to the bowl, and toss them with the mixture, making sure they are evenly coated.

Spread the potatoes on the prepared pan and bake for 22 to 25 minutes, or until cooked through and browned. Garnish with fresh dill and mustard seeds, if you wish.

3 tbsp (33 g) prepared spicy brown or Dijon mustard

2 tbsp (28 g) unsalted butter, ghee or coconut oil, melted (use oil for dairy-free)

2 tbsp (8 g) minced fresh dill

1 tsp salt

¼ tsp freshly ground black pepper

2 tsp (14 g) honey

4 cloves garlic, minced

1 tbsp (15 ml) coconut aminos

1½ lbs (680 g) small Yukon Gold potatoes, cut into quarters

Fresh dill and mustard seeds, for garnish (optional)

Better-for-You Plantain Fries

Paleo / Whole 30 Option / Egg Free / Gluten Free
Dairy Free / Nut Free / Vegan

I love using plantains because they are a versatile and inexpensive starch that adds variety to your plate. For baking purposes, I usually pick really ripe and sweet brown ones. For these fries, you actually want a semiripe, yellow plantain. They are slightly soft but just stiff enough to hold the fry shape and have a mild starchy flavor similar to potatoes. With these fries, the outside is crispy and the inside becomes a soft and enjoyable higher-fiber alternative to your typical potato or sweet potato.

Prep Time: 5 minutes
Cook Time: 25 minutes
Total Time: 30 minutes
Serves: 3 or 4

Preheat the oven to 425°F (220°C). Line a sheet pan with parchment paper.

Cut the plantains into fries and place in a medium bowl. In a small dish, mix together the salt, paprika, onion powder, cumin and coconut sugar.

Add the oil to the plantains and toss to coat. Add the spices to the bowl and toss again.

Spread the plantain fries in a single layer on the prepared pan.

Bake them for 22 to 25 minutes, until browned, flipping at about the 11-minute point. Garnish with scallions and serve with ketchup and guacamole for dipping, if you wish.

2 yellow plantains

½ tsp salt

¼ tsp paprika

¼ tsp onion powder

¼ tsp ground cumin

⅛ tsp coconut sugar (omit for Whole 30)

1½ tbsp (22 ml) coconut or olive oil

Chopped scallions, for garnish (optional)

Ketchup and guacamole, for serving (optional)

Sweet Potato–Cauliflower Mash

Egg Free / Gluten Free / Dairy-Free Option / Nut Free / Vegan Option

All potatoes are pretty dense and packed with carbohydrates. This recipe is a nice way to lighten the carbs on your plate without sacrificing the texture, while adding some extra hidden veggies to a family classic. If you're not a sweet potato fan, you can substitute any potato. Personally, I prefer the flavor profile of the traditional orange yam for this recipe. Just a few minutes of prep time and the whole recipe is done in 30 minutes.

Prep Time: 7 minutes
Cook Time: 23 minutes
Total Time: 30 minutes
Serves: 4

In a large saucepan, bring 6 cups (1.2 L) of water to a boil with ½ teaspooon of salt.

Add the potatoes and cauliflower to the boiling water. Cover and simmer until the potatoes are soft, about 15 minutes. Drain the water through a strainer once the potatoes are done.

Mash the vegetables and/or use an immersion blender, depending on how creamy you want them. If you want more of a puree, use an immersion blender.

Add ½ teaspoon of salt, the pepper, garlic, coconut oil, Greek yogurt, onion, coconut aminos, sage, rosemary and nutmeg. Stir to combine.

Top off with butter or coconut oil (for dairy free) and parsley, if you'd like, and serve.

1 tsp salt, divided

1 lb (455 g) sweet potatoes, peeled and chopped into 1-inch (2.5-cm) cubes

½ medium-sized head cauliflower, cut into florets

⅛ tsp freshly ground black pepper

1 clove garlic, minced

1 tbsp (14 g) coconut oil (if not necessary to be dairy-free, could sub unsalted butter or ghee), plus more for serving

2 tbsp (30 g) plain Greek yogurt (use dairy-free, if needed)

¼ cup (40 g) grated onion

2 tsp (10 ml) coconut aminos

¼ tsp ground sage

½ tsp minced fresh rosemary

Several dashes of freshly grated nutmeg

Chopped parsley, for garnish (optional)

Lighter Mango-Coconut Rice

Egg Free / Gluten Free / Dairy Free / Nut Free / Vegan Option

This recipe was inspired by the sticky rice I used to order at a small café called Playa del Mar in Costa Rica with my dad. I replaced half of the rice with cauliflower rice to lighten up the intensity of the richness as well as the sweetness from the coconut milk and mango. What I love about this recipe is that you can get the pleasant sweet and salty contrast in just 30 minutes. It pairs well with my Mango and Pineapple Chipotle Chicken (page 39) or a grilled white fish.

Prep Time: 8 minutes
Cook Time: 22 minutes
Total Time: 30 minutes
Serves: 4

In a medium-sized saucepan, combine the coconut milk, stock, mango puree, salt, cumin, paprika and turmeric and bring to a boil.

Add the rice and cauliflower rice, and return to a boil.

Cover the pan, lower the heat to medium-low and simmer for about 20 minutes, or until the rice is cooked. Leave the pan covered for 2 minutes after you turn off the heat, before serving. Top with avocado, mango, cilantro and red pepper flakes (if using).

Note: Rice cooking time can slightly vary. If it seems too al dente, simmer for a few more minutes until cooked to your liking.

1 cup (240 ml) full-fat coconut milk

1¼ cups (300 ml) chicken stock, chicken bone broth or veggie stock

⅓ cup (80 ml) mango puree (about ½ mango, peeled, pitted and blended until smooth)

¼ tsp salt

¼ tsp ground cumin

¼ tsp paprika

¼ tsp ground turmeric

1 cup (195 g) uncooked jasmine rice

1 cup (100 g) fresh or thawed frozen cauliflower rice

Optional Toppings
Chopped avocado
Chopped mango
Chopped fresh cilantro
Red pepper flakes

Tahini-Sesame
Sweet Potato Noodles

Paleo / Egg Free / Gluten Free / Dairy Free / Nut Free / Vegan Option

Tahini is a staple ingredient in many of my sauces, dips and baked goods. It has a neutral flavor compared to other nut and seed butters, with an ability to add creaminess to sauces and dressings. I find Asian noodle salads to be popular with my foodie following on Instagram and they are an enjoyable side. In this recipe, we replace the noodles with sweet potato noodles, making this recipe Paleo-friendly. This side is best paired with simple and less dressed proteins. In this quick recipe, the noodles require just 10 minutes of sautéing and the sauce takes only 5 minutes in a blender.

Prep Time: 5 minutes
Cook Time: 10 minutes
Total Time: 15 minutes
Serves: 4

In a large sauté pan, heat the coconut oil over medium heat and add the spiralized sweet potatoes. Cook until tender, about 10 minutes. Transfer the potatoes to a medium-sized bowl and set aside.

Meanwhile, in a high-speed blender, combine the water, tahini, lime juice, coconut aminos, maple syrup, sesame oil, sriracha to taste, ginger and salt, and blend until smooth.

Pour the sauce into a medium-sized bowl. For thinner consistency, add more water, 1 tablespoon (15 ml) at a time, and whisk.

Add the cabbage and bell pepper to the sweet potatoes, and toss to combine. Pour the sauce over the noodle mixture and toss again to combine. Garnish with cilantro, scallion and sesame seeds (if using). Serve.

2 tsp (10 g) coconut oil

2 medium-sized sweet potatoes, peeled and spiralized

1 tbsp (15 ml) water, plus more if needed

6 tbsp (90 g) unroasted or lightly roasted tahini

2 tbsp (30 ml) fresh lime juice

2 tbsp (30 ml) coconut aminos

1 tbsp (15 ml) pure maple syrup

1 tsp sesame oil

Sriracha

1 tsp grated fresh ginger

½ tsp salt

½ cup (45 g) shredded purple cabbage

¼ cup (38 g) seeded and chopped red bell pepper

Optional Garnish

Chopped fresh cilantro

Chopped scallion

Sesame seeds

Lightened-Up Creamy Potato Salad

Egg Free / Gluten Free / Nut Free

I find most potato salads lack flavor and are just not enticing when drenched in mayonnaise. Frankly, I don't enjoy it when I taste nothing but the mayo. I set out to design a recipe that has the creamy component of the traditional potato salad, but that is lighter and bolder in flavor. My potato salad uses a method of blending cottage cheese to create a creamy consistency. This recipe is light and fresh, adds a bunch of protein and is suitable for people with egg allergies.

Prep Time: 10 minutes
Cook Time: 15 minutes
Total Time: 25 minutes
(plus time to chill)
Serves: 8

In a large pot, cover the potatoes with water and add 1 teaspoon of salt. Cover the pot, bring the water to a boil and cook until the potatoes are tender, 12 to 15 minutes.

In a high-speed blender or food processor, combine the cottage cheese, sour cream, mustard, vinegar, honey, remaining salt, horseradish and pepper and blend until smooth. Scrape the mixture into a medium-sized bowl.

Add to the bowl, in this order, the chives, minced pickle, parsley and dill. Stir until well combined.

Place the mixture in the refrigerator to chill until ready to use.

Drain the potatoes and run them under cold water for about 30 seconds to cool them, then transfer the potatoes to a large bowl and fold the dressing mixture into the potatoes. Place in the refrigerator to chill until ready to serve, ideally 30 minutes or more. Garnish with chopped chives and red pepper flakes just before serving, if you'd like.

3 lbs (1.4 kg) red potatoes, chopped into 1-inch (2.5-cm) pieces

2 tsp (12 g) salt, divided

1½ cups (340 g) cottage cheese

¼ cup (60 g) sour cream

1 tbsp (11 g) prepared brown mustard

1 tbsp (15 ml) apple cider vinegar

1 tsp honey

¼ tsp prepared horseradish

⅛ tsp freshly ground black pepper

2 heaping tbsp (6 g) chopped fresh chives or (1 g) dried

2 tbsp (18 g) minced dill pickle

1 tbsp (4 g) chopped fresh parsley or (3 g) fresh cilantro

1 tbsp (4 g) chopped fresh dill

Optional Garnish
Chopped fresh chives
Red pepper flakes

Avocado Pesto Potato Salad

Paleo / Whole 30 / Egg Free / Gluten Free / Dairy Free / Vegan

I can smear pesto on just about any starchy food or protein. Of all of my pesto recipes, this is at the top of the list, because it is different from the traditional pesto that uses basil and pine nuts. Instead, I use cilantro, avocado and cashews to create a thick, creamy sauce that pairs deliciously with potatoes. This pesto was an experiment, to be honest, and it turned out to be very successful. This spin-off from your traditional potato salad is done in under 30 minutes. Bonus, this one is a good use for those leftover ripe avocados lying around.

Prep Time: 10 minutes
Cook Time: 15 minutes
Total Time: 25 minutes
(plus time to chill)
Serves: 8

Make the potatoes: In a large pot, cover the potatoes with water and add 1 teaspoon of salt. Cover the pot, bring the water to a boil and cook the potatoes until tender, 12 to 15 minutes.

Meanwhile, make the pesto: In a food processor, combine the avocado, cilantro, cashews, garlic, cumin, salt, pepper, lemon juice, coconut aminos and olive oil and process until smooth. Place the mixture in the refrigerator until ready to use.

Drain the potatoes and run them under cold water for about 30 seconds to cool them, then transfer the potatoes to a large bowl. Fold the pesto mixture into the potatoes. Place in the refrigerator to chill until ready to serve, ideally 30 minutes or more. Garnish with cilantro and red pepper flakes just before serving, if you'd like.

Potatoes

3 lbs (1.4 kg) Yukon Gold potatoes, chopped into 1-inch (2.5-cm) pieces

1 tsp salt

Pesto

1 ripe avocado, peeled and pitted

1 bunch cilantro, including stems, roughly chopped

½ cup (70 g) raw, unsalted cashews

3 cloves garlic, chopped

½ tsp ground cumin

¾ tsp salt

¼ tsp freshly ground black pepper

2 tbsp (30 ml) fresh lemon or lime juice

1 tbsp (15 ml) coconut aminos

3 tbsp (45 ml) olive oil

Optional Garnish

Fresh cilantro

Red pepper flakes

Roasted Winter Squash Medley

Paleo / Egg Free / Gluten Free / Dairy Free / Nut-Free Option / Vegan

Winter squash has a special place in my heart. "Squishy Squash," as my mother would call her signature dish, was my absolute favorite side dish that she prepared for Thanksgiving. She always added a touch of nutmeg, crushed Ritz crackers and butter. As I grew older and discovered the vast variety of winter squash, I was never satisfied with just one. From butternut, to acorn, to kabocha (my personal favorite), each squash has a unique way of complementing one another. This simple roasted medley is easy to prepare and serve in considerably less time than peeling, seeding, cutting and boiling winter squash in the traditional way. This recipe is ready in 30 minutes in the oven, or you can opt to air fry and save a few minutes.

Prep Time: 8 minutes
Cook Time: 22 minutes (for sheet pan method)
Total Time: 30 minutes
Serves: 6

Sheet Pan Method

Preheat the oven to 450°F (230°C). Place one or two sheet pans inside the oven to heat.

In a large bowl, combine the squash cubes with the melted oil. Add the coconut aminos, salt, pumpkin pie spice, pepper, onion powder and 1 teaspoon of the coconut sugar, and toss again.

Remove the sheet pans from the oven and line them with silicone sheets or parchment paper. Spread the squash evenly on the sheet pans; do not overcrowd.

Bake the squash for 15 minutes, then sprinkle with the remaining teaspoon of coconut sugar and toss. Bake for 4 more minutes.

Set the oven broiler to high, then place the pan 6 inches (15 cm) from the broiler and broil for 2 to 3 minutes, or until the tops begin to caramelize. To serve, add some crushed walnuts or pecans (if using).

Air Fryer Method

Preheat an air fryer to 370°F (188°C).

Follow the same steps as above to toss the squash with the seasoning.

Air fry (in batches if need be) for 10 minutes, then sprinkle the second teaspoon of coconut sugar and toss. Air fry for 2 or 3 more minutes, or until browned.

2½ lbs (1.1 kg) winter squash, peeled unless butternut, seeded and cut into small cubes (½" to ¾" [1.3 to 1.9 cm])

3 tbsp (45 g) coconut oil, melted

1 tbsp (15 ml) coconut aminos

¾ tsp salt

1 tsp pumpkin pie spice

¼ tsp freshly ground black pepper

½ tsp onion powder

2 tsp (10 g) coconut sugar, divided

Crushed walnuts or pecans, for serving (optional, omit for nut-free)

HEALTHY, FUN, SHAREABLE
Sweets

I am still moved when my fruit bowl is overflowing with overly ripe—nearly black—bananas. In fact, just the sight brings me back to getting ready to bake banana bread with my mother, the sweet aroma of banana, cinnamon and vanilla filling up the house. The anticipation I felt as an impatient child, my mouth watering, my senses overwhelmed, as I waited for the kitchen timer to sound. Let's be honest—when it comes to food, there is nothing like dessert to completely satisfy your cravings. I always wanted to be at the head of the line, ready to call dibs on that warm first slice. To this day, I still feel that same excitement, knowing my own freshly baked creations are about to be ready. Dessert is an everyday occurrence for me. It is my sin, and I enjoy every bite till the last!

When I was a kid, being the youngest had its perks! My parents were more laid back. For the most part, I could get away with murder. But more importantly, I received a lot more one-on-one time with my parents. Life kind of slowed down a bit. I imagine after raising twins (my brothers), I must have seemed like a saint . . . sorry, boys. I was able to learn many things as a child, but kitchen secrets were always my favorite and they had my undivided attention. The first baking lesson my mother ever taught me was how to make that delectable banana bread. We used lots of flour, butter, sugar and extra-black bananas, in most cases almost as black as this ink.

The loaves were gone in a matter of two days, tops. I'm pretty sure that, on more than one occasion, I ate it for every meal. Baking banana bread happened twice a year, Thanksgiving and Christmas, so I made sure to consume a fair share when I could.

I have a couple of decades of making my own banana bread recipes under me now. Through the years, I have created at least half a dozen versions. For this book, I chose my favorite one. It is simple. This recipe is gluten-free, made without refined sugar, and best of all, you would never know the difference! Just remember, the riper the bananas (think black ink), the better. I've also shared with you a few other childhood remakes: my Strawberries and Cream No-Bake Pie (page 152)—it's light, creamy and reminds me of a picnic at the park in the summer. I also rounded up my favorite cookie recipes, including Chewy Maple-Lemon Cookies (page 143), Oatmeal Cloud Cookies (page 155) and my Paleo and vegan Cinnamon Roll Cookies (page 159). And since I love dessert, I've included my favorite Single-Serve Avocado Chocolate Mug Brownie (page 151). Once the craving hits, there is nothing better than a personal-sized dessert in under 5 minutes! Everyone has their preferred indulgence, but you might need to try all of these before you pick your favorite.

Chewy Maple-Lemon Cookies

Paleo / Egg Free / Gluten Free / Dairy Free / Vegan Option

There's nothing that screams "dessert" like lemon . . . lemon squares, lemon meringue pie or, my favorite, lemon cake with lemon buttercream frosting. My recipe for lemon cookies has a crisp, yet chewy, almost toffee-like texture inside with a honey lemon icing that will melt in your mouth. This recipe is Paleo- and vegan-friendly, and complete in less than 25 minutes.

Prep Time: 10 minutes
Bake Time: 13 minutes
Total Time: 23 minutes
Makes: 10 to 12 cookies

Preheat the oven to 350°F (180°C). Line a sheet pan with parchment paper.

Make the cookies: In a large bowl, whisk together the almond flour, baking powder and salt.

In a separate bowl, combine the almond butter, maple syrup, vanilla extract and lemon zest. Mix until smooth.

Add the dry ingredients to the wet. Using a whisk, whisk very well until a thick batter forms (the batter at this point should seem very sticky and thick).

Using your hands, roll the batter into balls about 1½ tablespoons (about an inch [2.5 cm] in diameter) in size. They should not be sticky when you roll them. Place the balls about 3 inches (7.5 cm) apart on the prepared pan.

Place a small square of parchment paper over the first cookie. Using a flat-bottomed cup, gently flatten the cookie to about ¼ inch (6 mm) thick. Repeat for each cookie. Bake the cookies for 12 to 13 minutes. They should be slightly browned on the outside.

Meanwhile, make the icing: In a small bowl, combine the coconut oil, almond butter, lemon zest, salt, vanilla, lemon juice and honey, and whisk until smooth. Set aside.

Once the cookies are done baking, remove from the oven and transfer to a wire rack. Drizzle the icing over each cookie and allow to cool completely.

Cookies

½ cup (50 g) almond flour

½ tsp baking powder

⅛ tsp salt

½ cup (130 g) creamy almond butter

¼ cup (60 ml) pure maple syrup

1 tsp vanilla extract

1 tbsp (6 g) lemon zest

Icing

2 tbsp (28 g) coconut oil, at room temperature but not melted

1 tbsp (16 g) creamy almond butter

1 tsp lemon zest

Pinch of salt

⅛ tsp vanilla extract

1 tsp fresh lemon juice

2 tbsp (40 g) honey (use pure maple syrup for vegan)

Simple Healthy Banana Bread

Gluten Free / Dairy-Free Option

After years and years and hundreds of loaves made, nothing beats this simple banana bread recipe. I make these into mini loaves, which bake faster, in less than 30 minutes. You can absolutely make larger loaves; just be sure to alter the baking time as seen at the end of the recipe. This particular recipe is my favorite, using yogurt and applesauce. I have created a moist bread with a delicate crust sweetened with only a little added coconut sugar—I let the bananas do the talking. Oh, did I mention this recipe has no butter, no nuts and can be entirely gluten-free?

Prep Time: 5 minutes
Bake Time: 25 minutes
Total Time: 30 minutes
Makes: 6 mini loaves

Preheat the oven to 350°F (180°C). Oil 6 mini loaf pans (3¼ x 2½ inches [8.5 x 6.5 cm] per loaf).

In a medium-sized bowl, mix together the flour blend, oats, almond flour, cinnamon, baking soda and salt. Set aside.

In a stand mixer, combine the bananas, applesauce, coconut sugar, vanilla, yogurt and eggs, or use a large bowl and a hand mixer. Mix until smooth. Add the dry ingredients to the wet and mix again.

Divide the batter equally among the prepared mini loaf pans, each about three-quarters full. Top the loaves with the sliced banana (if using). Bake for 22 to 25 minutes, or until a toothpick inserted into the center of a mini loaf comes out clean. Remove from the oven, allow to cool and serve.

Note: If using regular small loaf pans (5¾ x 3 inches [14.5 x 7.5 cm] per loaf), bake for an additional 5 to 7 minutes.

Oil, for pans

1¼ cups (155 g) 1:1 gluten-free flour blend (I use King Arthur Measure for Measure)

¼ cup (20 g) old-fashioned oats (gluten-free, if needed)

2 tbsp (13 g) almond flour

1 tsp ground cinnamon

1½ tsp (7 g) baking soda

½ tsp salt

3 ripe bananas, mashed

¼ cup (60 g) applesauce

3 tbsp (42 g) coconut sugar

2 tsp (10 ml) vanilla extract

½ cup (115 g) Greek yogurt (dairy-free, if needed)

2 large eggs

Extra banana, sliced lengthwise (optional)

Warm Blueberry Crumble

Egg Free / Gluten Free / Dairy-Free Option / Vegan Option

Served warm, this vegan-friendly dessert can be served stand-alone or topped with vanilla ice cream or whipped cream (use dairy-free, if necessary). Prepped within 3 minutes on the stovetop in a cast-iron pan and finished off in the oven, this cozy dessert is ready to serve in 30 minutes. I love to use leftover crumble to top my pancakes and waffles for breakfast.

> Prep Time: 6 minutes
> Bake Time: 24 minutes
> Total Time: 30 minutes
> Serves: 6

Preheat the oven to 400°F (200°C).

Make the crumble: In a small bowl, combine the oats, almond flour, coconut sugar, applesauce, cinnamon and coconut oil. Stir until well mixed. Set aside.

Make the filling: Heat a 6- or 8-inch (15- or 20.5-cm) cast-iron (or any oven-safe) skillet over medium-high heat. Add the blueberries, lemon juice, maple syrup and potato starch and mix with a spoon. Cook for about 3 minutes, allowing the blueberries to release some of their liquid and thicken. Turn off the heat.

Top the filling with the crumble, place the skillet on the bottom rack of the oven and bake for 18 minutes. Then, place the skillet on the top rack and set the broiler to high. Broil for 3 minutes, or until the top gets nice and brown— be careful not to burn.

Remove the skillet from the oven. Top with your ice cream of choice.

Crumble

½ cup (40 g) old-fashioned oats (gluten-free, if needed)

¼ cup (25 g) almond flour

3 tbsp (42 g) coconut sugar

¼ cup (60 g) applesauce

½ tsp ground cinnamon

2 tbsp (28 g) coconut oil

Filling

4 cups (580 g) blueberries

1 tbsp (15 ml) fresh lemon juice

2 tbsp (30 ml) pure maple syrup

1 tbsp (9 g) potato starch or (8 g) cornstarch

For Serving

Ice cream (dairy or dairy-free, as desired)

Chocolate Banana Tart

Egg Free / Gluten Free / Dairy-Free Option / Vegan Option

Chocolate-covered bananas meet buttery shortbread—without the butter! This is a no-bake, vegan-friendly decadent dessert sure to be a fan favorite. Made in under 30 minutes, it takes less than 20 minutes to prep; just be sure to chill in the fridge for 4 hours before serving. This dessert keeps its quality and texture even after freezing.

Prep Time: 18 minutes
Cook Time: 5 minutes
Set Time: 4½ hours
Serves: 8 to 10

Make the crust: In a high-speed blender or food processor, combine the oats, cashews, coconut sugar and salt. Blend until the mixture becomes a fine powder. Transfer the mixture to a bowl, and add the coconut oil. Mix until a ball forms.

Press the ball into a circular baking pan or pie pan lined with parchment paper. Place the crust in the refrigerator for about 30 minutes. If you used a blender, clean it out to make the filling later.

Meanwhile, make the filling: In a medium-sized saucepan, heat the coconut milk and bananas together over medium-high heat and bring to a low boil. Lower the heat to medium and allow the bananas to soften for 3 to 4 minutes.

Remove the pan from the heat and transfer the warm bananas and milk to a clean high-speed blender. Blend until smooth.

Add the coconut oil, vanilla, cocoa powder, chocolate chips and agar agar. Blend the mixture again until smooth.

Remove the crust from the fridge. Pour the filling over the crust.

Refrigerate for at least 4 hours or overnight, until the tart has firmed up. Arrange the toppings on top of the tart however you'd like. Slice to serve.

Crust

1½ cups (120 g) old-fashioned oats (gluten-free, if needed)

1¼ cups (175 g) raw cashews

3 tbsp (42 g) coconut sugar

¼ tsp salt

4 tbsp (55 g) coconut oil, melted

Filling

1 (13.5-oz [400-ml]) can full-fat coconut milk (refrigerate overnight, remove the liquid and use only the solid cream)

2 ripe bananas, sliced

2 tbsp (28 g) coconut oil

1 tsp vanilla extract

2 tbsp (10 g) unsweetened cocoa powder

½ cup (88 g) chocolate chips (dairy-free, if needed)

1 tsp agar agar powder

Toppings

Sliced fresh figs or other fruit

Banana slices

Shaved chocolate

Granola or nuts

Single-Serve Avocado Chocolate Mug Brownie

Paleo / Egg Free / Gluten Free / Dairy-Free Option /
Keto Option / Vegan Option

In those moments when you need to satisfy your sweet tooth, what is better than a warm, fudgy brownie made in 5 minutes? This recipe uses avocado to achieve its decadent flavor. It is a cross between a mug cake and a molten lava cake. Serve it with a dash of whipped cream.

Prep Time: 3 minutes
Cook Time: 2 minutes
Total Time: 5 minutes
Serves: 1

In a mug, combine the coconut flour, almond flour and cocoa powder, and mix together with a fork.

Add the milk, vanilla, avocado and coconut sugar. Mix again until a smooth batter forms. It will be thick.

Stir in the chocolate chips. Microwave the mug on high for 1 minute and 45 seconds.

Top the mug cake with whipped cream (if using) and serve.

Note: Microwave oven powers may vary. You will know that the brownie is done when the top is slightly firm to touch in the center, but the chocolate chips will be melted inside the brownie.

1 tbsp (7 g) coconut flour

3 tbsp (19 g) almond flour

2 tbsp (10 g) unsweetened cocoa powder

2 tbsp (30 ml) milk of choice (dairy-free, if needed)

½ tsp vanilla extract

2 tbsp (18 g) mashed avocado

1 tbsp (14 g) coconut sugar (for a Keto-friendly option, use granulated monk fruit)

1 tbsp (11 g) chocolate chips (any chocolate chips will work; use dairy-free, if needed)

Whipped cream, for serving (optional; use dairy-free, if needed)

Strawberries and Cream No-Bake Pie

Egg Free / Gluten Free / Dairy-Free Option

An easy summertime dessert with no oven required, this recipe uses crispy brown rice cereal as the foundation for the crust. It sets up the delicate creamy top—soon to be a popular treat in your menu rotation. Prep this ahead of time in under 30 minutes, then let it chill for 3 to 4 hours before serving.

Prep Time: 10 minutes
Cook Time: 7 minutes
Set Time: 3–4 hours
Serves: 8

Cut a round piece of parchment paper to fit the base of a springform pan. Oil the sides of the pan.

In a small saucepan, combine the date syrup, coconut oil, almond butter, vanilla and salt. Heat over medium heat until well mixed and creamy.

In a large bowl, mix the crispy brown rice cereal with the warm mixture and use a wooden spoon to stir until it has the consistency of a crispy rice treat batter.

Pour the mixture into the prepared springform pan and press down with a spatula to pack it tightly. Place the pan in the freezer.

In a small bowl or mug, stir together the gelatin powder and water.

In a microwave, heat the jam in a microwave-safe mug for 45 seconds on high.

Add the jam to the gelatin mixture and whisk together until smooth. In a large bowl, combine the whipped topping and the gelatin mixture, and whisk until everything is combined. The color should be slightly pink. Next, add the yogurt and whisk again. Finally, fold in the strawberries.

Remove the crust from the freezer. Pour the strawberry mixture over the crust. Freeze the pie for 3 to 4 hours.

Remove the pie from the freezer. Using a butter knife, gently loosen the sides of the pan before releasing the spring. Carefully remove the sides of the pan. Top the pie with the sliced fresh strawberries, if you wish.

Note: If you don't have a springform pan, you could use a pie dish.

Oil, for pan

½ cup (120 ml) date syrup or pure maple syrup

2 tbsp (28 g) coconut oil

2 tbsp (32 g) almond butter

½ tsp vanilla extract

¼ tsp salt

4 cups (100 g) crispy brown rice or white rice cereal (gluten-free, if needed)

1½ tbsp (10 g) powdered beef gelatin or regular powdered gelatin

2 tbsp (30 ml) water, at room temperature

2 tbsp (40 g) no-added-sugar strawberry jam

1 (8-oz [226-g]) carton frozen whipped topping (dairy-free, if needed; I like to use coconut-based), thawed

¾ cup (173 g) Greek yogurt (dairy-free, if needed)

½ cup (85 g) chopped fresh strawberries

Extra sliced fresh strawberries, for topping (optional)

Oatmeal Cloud Cookies

Gluten Free / Dairy-Free Option / Nut Free

Oatmeal cookies for dessert? Count me in! My spin on this conventional favorite is using mashed white potatoes. Who would have thought using that instead of butter would produce such a soft, chewy and enjoyable cookie? This recipe takes 10 minutes of prep and about 15 minutes in the oven. Take an extra step and use these cookies to make the perfect ice cream sandwich. You won't regret it.

Prep Time: 10 minutes
Bake Time: 16 minutes
Total Time: 26 minutes
Makes: 24 cookies

Preheat the oven to 350°F (180°C). Line a sheet pan with parchment paper.

In a large bowl, mix together the oat flour, baking soda, salt and cinnamon.

In a separate bowl, mix together the mashed potato, coconut sugar, egg, tahini and vanilla until smooth.

Add the wet ingredients to the dry. Fold together, then mix until well combined. Fold in the chocolate chips.

Scoop 1½ tablespoon-sized balls (1 inch [2.5 cm] in diameter) and space about 2 inches (5 cm) apart on the prepared sheet pan. Gently flatten the balls with the back of an oiled fork.

Bake for 14 to 16 minutes, or until the tops are golden and edges are dry. Remove from the oven when done and transfer to a wire rack. Allow to cool completely.

2 cups (200 g) oat flour (gluten-free, if needed)

½ tsp baking soda

¼ tsp fine sea salt

1 tsp ground cinnamon

½ cup (113 g) boiled and then mashed white potato

½ cup (113 g) coconut sugar

1 large egg

¼ cup (60 g) tahini

2 tsp (10 ml) vanilla extract

¾ cup (131 g) dark chocolate chips (dairy-free, if needed)

Oil, for oiling the fork

No-Bake Raspberry
Dark Chocolate Bites

Paleo / Egg Free / Gluten Free / Dairy-Free Option / Vegan

A light dessert where dark chocolate marries raspberry with an added crunch. These bites are perfect after an indulgent dinner when you need to satisfy that sweet tooth without the guilt. This vegan-friendly recipe comes together within 10 minutes.

Prep Time: 10 minutes
Bake Time: 0 minutes
Total Time: 10 minutes
Makes: 12 to 14 bites

In a food processor, combine the cashews, coconut flour and salt, and pulse about 8 times.

Next, add the almond butter, vanilla, dates and coconut oil. Pulse about 5 times.

Finally, add the raspberries and pulse until all the ingredients are well mixed and a thick "dough" forms.

Transfer to a medium-sized bowl. Add the chopped chocolate, and using clean hands, incorporate the chocolate into the mixture. Roll the mixture into balls about 1 inch (2.5 cm) in diameter. Store in the fridge or freezer.

1½ cups (210 g) raw cashews

¼ cup (28 g) coconut flour

¼ tsp salt

¼ cup (64 g) creamy or crunchy almond butter

½ tsp vanilla extract

7 pitted dates, chopped

1 tbsp (14 g) coconut oil or ghee (use oil for dairy-free), at room temperature

2.5 oz (70 g) freeze-dried raspberries (½ cup)

1.5 oz (43 g) dark chocolate, chopped (any chocolate will work; use dairy-free, if needed)

Cinnamon Roll Cookies

Paleo / Egg Free / Gluten Free / Dairy-Free Option / Vegan

I love a good snickerdoodle, but in most cases the cinnamon gets lost in the flavor profile. My focus with this recipe was to allow the cinnamon to shine. Simply made with six ingredients, this crunchy, vegan-friendly cookie has all the flavors of a cinnamon roll.

Prep Time: 15 minutes
Bake Time: 14 minutes
Total Time: 29 minutes
Makes: 12 to 14 cookies

Preheat the oven to 350°F (180°C). Line a sheet pan with parchment paper.

Make the dough: In a medium-sized bowl, combine the almond flour, almond milk, coconut sugar and vanilla. Using a fork, mix well until a ball of dough forms. Roll the dough into a cylinder about 6 inches (15 cm) in length, and wrap with parchment paper. Place the dough in the freezer to freeze for 5 to 10 minutes (the longer you freeze, the easier the slicing will be).

Meanwhile, make the filling: In a small bowl or mug, combine the coconut oil, coconut sugar and cinnamon until a paste forms.

Remove the dough from the freezer and place it on a piece of parchment paper. Cover the dough with a second piece of parchment paper, and using a rolling pin, flatten the to form a rectangle approximately 9 x 4 inches (23 x 10 cm).

Spread the filling evenly over the dough, leaving a ¼-inch (6-mm) border on the long side of the rectangle. Using a long, sharp knife, carefully lift the edges of one long side of the rectangle up, releasing it from the parchment paper. Curl the lifted edge into the dough to begin tightly rolling it into a long cinnamon roll. The dough will be sticky. Use the parchment paper to make each individual rolling motion, peel it back, away from the side of the roll, then repeat until you have a long roll. Carefully seal the edge by pressing together gently.

Using a sharp, wet knife, slice the roll into ½-inch (1.3-cm) slices; you will have 12 to 13 slices. You can carefully round the edges if the cookies have flatted from the slicing. Place the slices on the prepared pan. Use one small piece of parchment paper to cover one cookie, and flatten using the flat bottom of a cup. Repeat for each cookie. Bake for 14 minutes, or until the edges are golden brown in color.

While the cookies bake, make the icing: In a small saucepan, heat the coconut butter, maple syrup, cinnamon, vanilla and salt over low heat just until warm enough to mix together. Remove from the heat and set aside.

Remove the pan from the oven and transfer the cookies to a wire rack to cool. Drizzle a little icing over each cookie. Allow to set before serving.

Dough

1 cup (100 g) almond flour

2 tbsp (30 ml) almond milk

3 tbsp (42 g) coconut sugar

½ tsp vanilla extract

Filling

2 tbsp (28 g) coconut oil or ghee (use oil for dairy-free), at room temperature

2 tbsp (28 g) coconut sugar (can sub raw cane sugar for non-Paleo)

1 tsp ground cinnamon

Icing

¼ cup (55 g) culinary coconut butter (not coconut oil—you can find this in most grocery stores in the natural foods section, at Whole Foods, or on Amazon)

2 tbsp (30 ml) pure maple syrup

¼ tsp ground cinnamon

¼ tsp vanilla extract

Pinch of salt

Acknowledgments

I have to start by thanking my family. Mom, George, Colleen, Michael and John, thank you for all the memories. Writing these recipes took me down memory lane and I was reminded how special each of you are and of the time we have spent together. Dad, I wish you were here, but know that your spirit guided me through.

Thank you to my love, Tony. From reading early drafts to sitting with me for hours on end while I wrote descriptions to testing recipes, you have always been there encouraging me to challenge myself. Your contribution was essential to this project, and I will always be grateful to you for that. You have been my biggest support, my cheerleader . . . always giving me the push or the hug that I needed. Thank you for your patience, and thank you for being my best friend. I love you so much, babe.

Thank you, Nichole. You have truly made a significant impact on me as a person as well as my business over the last year and a half. You are not just an integral part of my brand's team, but you have become an amazing friend. You can always put a smile on my face and change my perspective. I am grateful for all you do.

Thank you, Helen. I wouldn't have been able to balance all of my work without your help formatting recipes, editing drafts and always providing me with helpful feedback. I am blessed to have had you on my team throughout this process.

Thanks to everyone from Page Street, who helped me so much. Special thanks to my editor, Sarah, for always taking the time to hear my ideas and guide me along the way. I most certainly could not have done any of this without you!

Thank you to each and every one of you, my Instagram and blog community. Your support is the reason I am here today sharing my recipes and making my dreams come true. You are not just my audience; you are my friends and my family. I look forward to my job because of each and every one of you, and I love you from the bottom of my heart.

A special thank you to all my personal recipe testers. Mom, Colleen and Arash, your time, love and input was more valuable than you'll ever know. You are the best.

To my entire circle of family and friends who have supported me throughout my life, helped me face my challenges and have impacted the person I am today. Mom and George, thanks for always supporting my dreams and for all of your love and guidance. To my siblings, I'm so grateful to have three siblings I can also call friends. Each of you has impacted the person I am today. To my in-laws, my friends (you are my family), my extended family, I am blessed with an incredible circle of people in my life. Diana and Stacey, thank you for helping me find my spirit. Thank you Vicky, Charlene, Karen, Melissa, Alexie, Jenna, Nicole, Briana, Kathy, Pat, Janet and Pete, and Steve. To all of the amazing kids in my life: Izza, Anthony, Xavier, Miles, Riley, Rowen, Keegan, thanks for being lights in my life. A special thanks to Lou and Dean for being my youngest and biggest fans. And to everyone else in my life, you know who you are. I love you.

About the Author

Caitlin Greene is the founder of Star Infinite Food, a blog that started out as a personal journey. After years of living with an eating disorder, Caitlin made a commitment to heal her disordered relationship with food. She used Instagram as a platform to hold herself accountable throughout her recovery, and in 2016, her blog was born. She began publicly sharing her recipes made with simple ingredients and whole foods. The content that Caitlin shared quickly gained traction on Instagram, and within a couple of years she had several thousand followers. Her dedication to real-food ingredients and passion for creating recipes and styling food led to her full-time career as a food blogger. Caitlin grew up in a family of cooks and has been in the kitchen since she was five years old. She enjoys inspiring others with her colorful meals by showing that healthy food can be exciting and easy.

 @starinfinitefood

Index